SO-AZR-162

O UGHTEN
H OUSE
P UBLICATIONS

"Books and Tools for the Rising Planetary Consciousness"

NAVIGATING THE '90s

A step-by-step guide to rising above the
confusion and chaos to gain clarity
in the most intense times ever.

by Deborah Soucek

Edited by Sara Benjamin-Rhodes

Published by
Oughten House Publications
Livermore, California
USA

NAVIGATING THE '90s

A STEP-BY-STEP GUIDE TO RISING ABOVE THE CONFUSION AND CHAOS TO GAIN CLARITY IN THE MOST INTENSE TIMES EVER.

© 1995, 1996 by Deborah Soucek
Published 1995. Second Edition 1996.

00 99 98 97 96   0 9 8 7 6 5 4 3 2

SECOND EDITION

All rights reserved. No part of this book may be reproduced or transmitted, or translated in any form or by any means, electronic or mechanical, including photocopying, recording, or by any information storage and retrieval system, except for inclusion of brief quotations in a review, without permission in writing from the publisher. The publisher and author are most willing to work with interested parties, provided that proper procedures are followed.

DESIGN BY DAVID CHO, CHO & ASSOCIATES, LOS ANGELES, CALIFORNIA

EDITED BY SARA BENJAMIN-RHODES

PUBLISHED BY:
OUGHTEN HOUSE PUBLICATIONS
P.O. BOX 2008
LIVERMORE, CALIFORNIA, 94551-2008 USA

Library of Congress Cataloging-in-Publication Data
Navigating the '90s: a step-by-step guide to rising above the confusion
    and chaos to gain clarity in the most intense times ever
    Deborah Soucek
        p.   cm.
    ISBN 1-880666-47-2 (alk. paper) $13.95
    1. Conduct of life. 2. Self-help techniques. 3. Self-actualization
    (Psychology) I. Soucek, Deborah 1949- . II. Title.
    BJ1581.2.S636   1996
    158--dc20   95-46005
                                                    CIP

ISBN 1-880666-47-2, Trade Publication
                Printed in United States of America
            Printed with vegetable ink on acid-free paper

Acknowledgment

Special thanks to Cheri Billups and "The Tuesday Group," the first test group to meet weekly and incorporate this material into their daily lives. Their courage and subsequent growth and change have been the highest form of validation imaginable.

Publisher's Note

We at Oughten House extend our wholehearted appreciation and gratitude to each of our Literary Producers for making this publication possible: Marge and John Melanson, Barbara Rawles, Robin Drew, Irit Levy, Debbie Detwiler, Kiyo Monro, Alice Tang, Eugene P. Tang, Brad Clarke, Victor Beasley, Ruth Dutra, Nicole Christine, Dennis Donahue, Fred J. Tremblay, Kathy Cook, Debbie Soucek, and Kimberley Mullen.

TABLE OF CONTENTS

Lesson 1. Be aware of judgment.

Lesson 2. Honor yourselves.
>> What brings you joy?
>> What makes you "you"?
>> The benefits of meditation

Lesson 3. "Body language"
>> How your body assists you in the decision making process
>> Literal body messages

Lesson 4. You are what you believe.
>> Learning about your "web of beliefs"

Lesson 5. Watch what you say.
>> Words that restrict your actions and self-image

Lesson 6. I didn't hear you.
>> Develop clear communications.
>> Learn about cores of "necessary information"

Lesson 7. You're right on schedule.
>> Slow down and relax!
>> No wrong decisions

TABLE OF CONTENTS (cont.)

Lesson 8. Who loves you, baby?

Discernment and the fear factor

Process information in your own time

Love masqueraders

Lesson 9. Breathe easy.

Daily "triggers" that create stress
and how your breathing can make a
difference

Lesson 10. Garbage in, garbage out

How foods affect your body and
your awareness

Lesson 11. No victims, please!

Take action to stop the victim cycle

Don't settle for less

Lesson 12. Change and Control

The illusion of control

Why change is growth

Lesson 13. Complain, complain, complain!

How complaining lowers self-esteem
and how it affects the body

Lesson 14. Eliminate your need to justify.

How justifying is complaining in disguise

Lesson 15. Buddy, can you spare a dime?

Money and your financial belief system

TABLE OF CONTENTS (cont.)

Lesson 16. Growing Pains
> A look at adolescence

Lesson 17. Wait a minute! Wait a minute!
> Procrastination

Lesson 18. Square Pegs
> How feelings of not fitting in
> can benefit you now

Lesson 19. Where is love?
> Discerning loving behaviors and
> their many disguises

Lesson 20. Asking for help
> How not to be overwhelmed

Lesson 21. All work and no play
> Redefining "work"

Lesson 22. Thanks, but "No thanks!"
> Recurring unpleasant situations and
> what they offer

Lesson 23. Share and share alike.
> Confusing messages in sharing and
> group mind-sets

Lesson 24. That's entertainment!
> The effects of imprinting

Lesson 25. Manifest destiny.
> You deserve your dreams

PREFACE

Navigating the '90s is a compilation of the basic lessons I received from my teacher, Jason Manyfeathers. In short, I call this work "the Jason lessons."

Since 1985, I have been happy to be Jason's student. His teachings have helped me survive and thrive in the fast-paced, deadline-driven profession of advertising and marketing. Jason's lessons seemed to simplify my complex and hectic world and give meaning where none had existed before.

Jason showed me how I complicated my own life, out of conditioned, ignorant choices that I wasn't aware that I was making. He showed me that life is truly simple and joyful. And his lessons moved "theoretical" concepts (that I thought I already "knew") out of my head and into the practical reality of my daily life, where I could see them work and produce results.

So, if you're looking for results in your life, I offer these lessons to you.

Jason says the learning does not come from the words, but from putting the lessons into practice. It is his hope that you will share these lessons — and more importantly, your "homework" and subsequent realizations — on a weekly basis with your friends, family, co-workers or other appropriate small group. Your collective and reciprocal sharing of how you all include these lessons into your daily lives will offer the *experience* of the true teaching and wisdom.

Although these lessons are told through me, the words are Jason's. As such, I hope you will be able to feel Jason's concern, wisdom, and humor. This book is truly a guidebook for enjoying these hectic and challenging times!

FOREWORD

My dear friends,

I know many of you have questions, confusion, and anxiety right now. Understand that this is one of the most remarkable times ever on the planet. As much as it will be incredibly wonderful, it will also appear to be incredibly stressful, chaotic, and terrifying at times. This is the most concentrated time ever on Earth.

You are reacting to all the preliminary (physical) forces and you are quite sensitive. The fact that you are reading this now attests to the fact that you are attuned to the changes, the new paradigm or whatever you may wish to call the times we will be evolving to. I know there are many voices predicting and foretelling the times ahead. You are literally being bombarded now, not just with information from many cultures on the planet, but also from many different energy sources.

This is an interesting time for many reasons. You have all chosen to be here now, though you cannot remember all the reasons why. This is the intergalactic show of all times, and it will certainly be worth the wait for you all. At present, you cannot imagine all the wonders to come.

I know there are two "camps" forming now, not just in your country, but around the globe: those who are sucked into fear-based realities and those who are grounded in love. I know this can sound simplistic — especially from my perspective — but, in essence, things *are* very simple. This is one of the lessons I hope to teach.

This is not a time for frantic thoughts and erratic actions. This is a time of celebration, purification, of opening to the wonders of a loving universe that have been kept from you for eons. This is a time for truth, beauty, and wisdom. And all from within yourselves.

Many of you have started to move toward your inner guidance, although you may not be able to articulate that that is what your restless movement is, just yet. And I know the words, "have faith" have been overused in your society, but that is what I am asking each of you to do.

So, in short, the most important thing you can do in these trying and wonderful times is to make time for yourselves. Make time for meditation and relaxation. Make time to honor the unarticulated hunches or feelings you are having.

It will be very helpful to keep a journal now. Not just to chronicle the day's events, but to actually manifest your thoughts and elusive feelings onto paper with pen. This will validate the "wispy" thoughts and vague feelings you will be receiving. Keeping a journal will also aid in showing you how fast you are progressing in the months ahead.

You have all traveled so far. You are to be congratulated. You may think of your life and these times as a great treasure hunt. Without ever being told, you knew in what direction to go, which books to read, what seminars to attend, and what teachings to discount. Do not make light of this. This is not coincidence. You have followed all the clues and you are now in sight of the treasure. And as you well know, the majority of humanity isn't even aware that there even is a hunt in progress!

Know that you are a leader. The time has come to change from the role of student to the role of teacher. Know that you have volunteered to teach your brethren to slowly wake up in the coming months. Many of you have already been doing this, and more will follow.

But as important as it will be to impart the vast amounts of teachings coming in, *it is also imperative to <u>teach</u> and not to <u>preach</u>!*

Know that the difference between teaching and preaching is who asks the first question. It's that simple.

For example, rather than asking someone, "Would you like to hear about a new book I've been reading?" simply state (to someone you feel may be receptive), "I've been reading a rather interesting book." IF the answer is "Oh, really? What is it about?" then proceed. Let the *listener* ask the questions; let the *listener* ask you for the teaching. Otherwise, your words will fall on deaf ears, and the time is too short to tolerate the waste and ill effects of New Age "preachers" telling their friends how they can fix them.

Understand that not everyone will be ready to be your student. You must discern who is ready to learn. *They will ask you!* They will sense something in you that they need and they will seek you out. Be sensitive to this.

Sometimes the most unlikely candidates will ask you. This will be a challenge for you to be honest and supportive and to learn how much information you will wish to impart, but I know you will all enjoy the task.

Also, don't think that if you aren't giving seminars for hundreds of people that you aren't doing your job. That's hogwash! If you impart your message to just one person and help that person to grow, you've been extremely successful in your role as a teacher.

Please do not take any of our words lightly (although at times we will do our best to "lighten you up," with our version of humor and playfulness).

These words are delivered in a precise cadence that will trigger patterns long since buried in your beings. Know that the structure and the cadence of the words also convey meaning to you on a subconscious level, as well. In a sense, you are being infused with the messages. You may just "get" ideas without having to struggle with them on an intellectual level. Or you may enjoy the lexiconigraphical aerobics as well, if that is your personality.

It will also be helpful to re-read these passages — not only while you are reading them for the first time, to "drink in" all the subtleties, but to re-read them after some time has passed since reading the entire piece. You will receive as much information on the second reading as you will on the first.

So, before we can embark on our journey, perhaps we need to be speaking the same language. Words are so powerful in your world! I will attempt to "re-define" some basic concepts so we may all "play off the same sheet of music," so to speak.

It is with the utmost love and respect that I present these ideas to you. Know that the chapters are structured as lessons, as this is a familiar format to you. However, understand that doing the lessons in sequence and doing the "homework" is IMPERATIVE for you to gain the full effect of the lessons. This will enable you to incorporate the teachings immediately into your daily routine, and will actually manifest their essences into physical form.

With that said, it's time to start "school."

— Jason

"Once you become sensitized to the extent of

judgments around you,

you will be aware as you encounter them.

Then you can alter their purpose."

———◆———

Lesson 1

Rise above societal conditioning.
Be aware of judgment.

My dearest friends,

Cease to judge yourselves and be critical. I know that being a member of a society where judgment is related to every aspect of daily life is most difficult. You are so conditioned to judge everything: your clothes, your hair, your car, your performance in your work, your political figures (though this may be warranted), your recreation (your golf game), and your entertainment (rating movies on a scale from one to ten) — just to name a few. I've even heard that you have "fashion police," to deal with those who do not dress as some would wish!

Please know that all aspects of judgment are as insignificant as the need for "fashion police." So from this point forward, be aware of how much judgment is a part of your daily life. You may even want to keep a journal of your thoughts and conversations, to begin with. You may wish to note what you read in the newspaper, hear on the radio, on television, from friends, co-workers, family members, and others with whom you come in contact on a daily basis, to become aware of the EXTENT you are surrounded by judgments. It may surprise you.

Know that this "culture of judgment" — and it truly is that — is addictive and manipulative. It will also keep you from progressing in your growth. Think of this environment of judgment as shackles on your legs. It is time to break free and have no limits.

So, how do you do that? Start with the simple elements. Only read the articles in a newspaper you need to read. Listen to music only in your cars (tapes or CDs you enjoy, for example). Turn off the commentary and be carefully selective of the information you invite into your life.

Once you become sensitized to the extent of judgments around you, you will be aware of them as you encounter them. Then you can alter their purpose. For example, if you are in a conversation with someone and they mention something like, "Can you believe that jacket so-and-so is wearing?" you can actually nip this in the bud by saying something like, "Actually, I think it is quite beautiful — what a wonderful color!" Or if someone says, "I saw a movie that was absolutely awful!" You might reply, "Really? I've heard from others who enjoyed it, but I guess it was not to your liking." *That is taking a judgment and returning it to a preference.*

In short, taking an attitude of:

That's good
That's bad
That's awful

and returning it to:

I enjoyed it
I appreciate it
It's not to my liking
I'm not sure I understand it.

It's the difference between making statements or sweeping generalizations that include a judgment and being specific about how YOU perceive it or feel about it.

Not only will this new way of approaching information "move you forward," but it will be a powerful way you can "re-train" others in a subtle and loving way.

Your assistance in this will help to shift the paradigm more quickly, will start to wake up people to learn the power of their words, to not just act and react on "auto pilot."

Homework assignment:

In your journal, keep a list for the next two weeks: Note all the elements of judgment you encounter throughout the day (articles you read in the paper, the tone of a TV story, the shows you watch, the movies you see, and the conversations you have). Be as detailed as possible.

At the end of those two weeks, answer the following questions:

1. What have I learned from this period of observation? To what extent do I encounter judgment in my daily life?

2. What actions am I taking (will I take) to alter my daily life?

3. How have I begun to subtly show others what I am learning?

After you have completed the above, please continue to note items 2 and 3 in your journal, on an ongoing basis. Having these results on paper will be VERY beneficial to you!

"Most adults today are running

strictly on 'auto pilot.'

We need to get you back to your

manual controls."

———•◆•———

Lesson 2

Honor yourselves.

Once you start to disengage from the daily conditioning of your society, you will also begin to learn your true value and true identity.

Know that there is so much "programming" surrounding you that defines your value and identity, such as your profession, social class, educational level, and so on. These areas have absolutely nothing to do with your identity. And it will be difficult to honor yourself if you are not aware of who you are.

Who are you, apart from your job, family, circle of friends, or heritage? What is the essence that makes you "you"? Underneath the programming, the judgment, and the expectations *is a perfect being ... you!* But how do you, first of all, believe that to be true, and then how do you get in touch with that wonderful essence that *is* you?

Because there is so much programming from all your outside areas of influence, it will actually take *getting in touch with your wonderful essence to believe it exists*!

And the one way to do that is to meditate.

If you already meditate on a daily level, you know the importance of this powerful tool. If you do not, you cannot imagine the gifts in store for you.

Firstly, if you are not presently meditating daily, please begin. It is always best to find a teacher — one who currently practices daily. There are many forms of meditation, and you may wish to try several, to find the one that works best for you. Transcendental meditation is only one method. Meditation is not just for yogis. The purpose of meditation is to alter the breath, to alter your consciousness, enabling you to reach a state where you can "tune out" the outside influences that so rule your daily life.

Meditation also stimulates the pineal and pituitary glands, and will cause a hormonal reaction to evoke a state of relaxation and bliss. With your world growing increasingly hectic and stressful, you will welcome this "instant vacation."

Know that by the time you reach adulthood, you are so out of touch with your innate spirit, it may seem foreign. From day one, you are taught how to think, how to act, how to react to every set of circumstances and stimuli. Most adults today are running strictly on "auto pilot." We need to get you back to your manual controls.

So, the first way to learn to honor yourself is to get in touch with the essence that is you. So please put aside at least twenty minutes a day to meditate and close out the outside world. This will give you the clarity, not only to learn of your inner strengths and wisdom, but to enable you to perform better in your job, help you to make more informed decisions, and to act and not to just react to your life.

The second way to get in touch with your essence is to learn which are the things in life that bring you joy, which would make your spirit alive and bring a smile to your face. So many of you find yourselves in lives and situations that do not reflect your passions and your innate talents. So, you need to find all the things that make you feel good and, in turn, increase the flow of energy within you.

Homework:

1. Meditate twenty minutes a day. Keep a journal to record your feelings and insights from meditation. If you do not already know how to meditate, find a teacher, a book, or a video that will help you.

Consult your health insurance plan, stress management practitioners, New Age bookstores and magazines, continuing adult education — even health food stores will be able to help you get a start if you don't know where to look. Believe me, this is the greatest gift you can give yourself, bar none!

2. Make a list of all the things you LOVE to do. Take your time. You may even want to keep adding to the list over a week's time. What are the things in life that make you feel alive, that give you a sense of incredible happiness, where you totally can forget the outside world?

3. If you had all the money and time to do anything, what would you do? After you had time to rest, upgrade your comfort level and so on, how would you choose to spend your days? What type of people would you choose to surround yourself with? What would you do to interact with people? What have you always wanted to pursue, but didn't have the training, the time, or the money to do?

Make a list. Again, take as long as you need to make this complete. These three areas will begin to give you an idea of who you are in truth: your identity, your power, and your sensitivities.

Once you know your truth, you can begin to live your truth. Then life becomes so much more exciting!

More later, but for now, class dismissed.

"There is no such thing as a hard decision to make.

Your body always makes it first."

———————

Lesson 3

"Body language"

Now that you have a clearer understanding of your identity, you have a better understanding of all the things that bring you joy. This awareness will help you literally *feel* what is best for you and will be invaluable in your decision-making process.

In other words, if you are faced with a decision, drop your awareness from your mind into your feeling center, around the solar plexus. You will sense that one solution is more pleasant than the other. One solution will give you a tinge of fear, which you can actually feel. One solution will bring more joy.

Now, your first reaction may be that you are taking the "easy way out," by deciding on the option which makes you feel better. In short, that is true. But the emphasis is on what makes your BODY feel better. Your body is your greatest teacher. Listen to its messages.

You have cycles throughout the day, times when your concentration is greater, when you are more "hyper," when you are more conceptual and creative, and so on. You will receive messages throughout the day about the tasks you want to do next. Your first reaction may be that you are "lazy," and are avoiding the difficult tasks, but this is usually not the case. (And then, there ARE some tasks to be avoided!)

Nobody — no one — can tell you better than your body what is best for you. I know this is difficult to "swallow" in a culture where your doctors are revered as gods, and where health care has nothing to do with true healing.

So, learn what upsets your body and what makes your body feel comfortable.

You may not like to hear this, but your greatest traumas and greatest crises are always your greatest teachers, especially when you tune in to your body.

Your body is very wise. It performs well for you constantly. Return the respect and devotion. You, after all, are quite close to your body, are you not?

Have you ever walked into a room or an elevator, saw a person you did not know, and your body immediately felt uncomfortable? Perhaps a knot in your stomach? Stop thinking of these occurrences as "weird" and understand that your body knows more than you. Or, more appropriately, your body *remembers* more than you do.

So, in short, there is no such thing as a hard decision to make. Your body always makes it first. Just listen for the cues and you'll not only find the entire decision-making process easier and faster, but your body will feel less stress and discomfort, and respond favorably in thanks.

"Literal messages" —

On a somewhat larger scale, your body may talk with you very plainly, but your culture has forgotten to listen. Now, to get your attention, your body will attempt to send a literal message to you, which you interpret as pain. This actually becomes amusing.

For example, your back aches. This may be a literal message that you are not feeling supported, as your spine (the element that supports your entire skeletal structure) is "speaking." Or it may mean that you need more "backbone." But ask your body what message it is sending and it will reply! It's really very simple! Or, for example, if you have diarrhea, you are literally getting rid of [waste]. Ear infections may be telling you that there is something you do not wish to hear. Legs/knees may tell you that you do not want to move forward, do not want movement of any kind (change), or want to slow your pace down.

The more you listen to your body, the more "in tune" with it you will become. And when you take action on the body's initial messages, you eliminate the need for more drastic messages or dis-eases.

Homework:

1. In your journal, keep a listing of decisions you make on a day-to-day basis: where to go, what to eat, who to socialize with, or when to do your specific work tasks. Write down your options and what body reactions you had to each. Also write down any "chatter" that may be occurring in your head, telling you why you shouldn't listen to your body.

2. Make a note of any reactions your body has to people you meet for the first time. Be sensitive to this. This will be an incredible asset to you in your daily life. Then enter additional information about that person as you become aware of it.

3. If you have a particularly difficult situation you are dealing with, take some time to meditate on what the greater lessons for you are. Write this down in your journal. This will be INVALUABLE as you move through periods of confusion and wavering back and forth.

4. Keep an ongoing list of "literal" body messages: the "symptom" you feel, the severity and duration, and the reason your body is telling you it needs your attention.

Again, *writing this information down* will bring much information to your *conscious* attention.

Class dismissed.

"You are a result of your beliefs.

How you look, what you do for a living,

who you admire and, more importantly,

who you disdain."

———◆———

Lesson 4

You are what you believe.

Once you are more in touch with your body and its messages, you will be better able to understand how your societal "programming" has created your beliefs, and — in short — your reality, but not your truth.

Understand that *beliefs are*, in short, "mantras," or *verbal "keys" to program the mind*. And your world is FULL of "beliefs" that have nothing to do with truth!

Once upon a time, there were many people who believed the world to be flat. That was their reality at that time. But it was (and is) not the truth.

As an example, let's say that from the time you were a child, you were told that if you were to go outside in the rain, you would catch cold. And anytime that you may have been caught in a rainstorm — even briefly, walking to your car or cab — you (sure enough!) caught cold the next day!

Understand that this is not truth. It is the reality you've created. This is programming your mind to catch cold *after* you've been in the rain *because you were told this was an absolute truth!* There are many people who *can* go out in the rain and never catch cold from it, because they don't believe that false dogma.

If this applies to the weather's affects on the body, imagine how infused you are with messages from your media, from your interactions at work, from your family — on a *daily* basis!

How many spiders have been stepped on because people have been told from the time they were toddlers that spiders are bad (a judgment), and therefore have no right to live? Frankly, more of your species have performed heinous acts than spiders have. And though you may not necessarily LIKE spiders, the automatic reaction that some of you have when you see one is based on a conditioned belief, not on truth.

But this is not about rain, a flat Earth, or spiders. This is about you and your life. You are a result of your beliefs: how you look, what you do for a living, who you admire, and, more importantly, who you disdain.

Think of prejudice (to "pre-judge"). How many people have negative feelings toward different groups of people, based on their homeland, different customs, different values, and different ways of relating to situations. This is not truth, though it may be some people's reality. *All* people are valuable. Everyone has value. But judgment and beliefs are often intertwined.

Many of you (and especially you "boomers") are breaking through much multigenerational programming of your beliefs and are to be congratulated. You are understanding how family dysfunctionality creates behaviors (and beliefs) that can be changed! You are not passing along behaviors to your children that you no longer believe to be valid! Bravo!

So, how do you tell a "belief" from a "truth"? Simple. Does anyone believe the opposite to be true? Take the abortion issue, for example. Each side has a totally different *belief* which creates a totally different reality — not to mention judgment!

And without judging either side, understand that anytime ANY issue is so hotly and emotionally contested, it is engineered (intentionally) to separate you, to create fear. But more on that later.

Homework:

1. In your journal, keep an ongoing record of hotly debated issues which you find highlighted in the media. Note how each side has its own perception of reality.

2. When you react with guilt or sadness to something, ask yourself what it is that you believe that evokes that emotion. THIS WILL BE INVALUABLE TO PUT IN WRITING.

3. Complete the following sentences with what you currently believe about yourself and your reality:

I believe I am:

I believe I am:

I believe I am:

I believe I am:

I believe I am not:

I believe I am not:

I believe I am not:

I believe I am not:

I believe the world is:

I believe these times are:

I believe my life is:

I believe my childhood was:

I believe women are:

41

I believe men are:

I believe children are:

I believe animals are:

I believe: (Write about your other beliefs.)

Know that what you've written above — no matter how positive — will limit and define you. Do you know (or know of) other people who have different beliefs? Many times different beliefs will separate people, cultures, races, countries, and age groups. Become aware of other people's beliefs (if they are different from yours) and be tolerant. This practice of tolerance will give you a powerful influence with those you encounter.

"I am always amazed how people

in your culture are trained

to disrespect themselves."

———⊷◆⊶———

Lesson 5

Watch what you say.

I've alluded to the fact that words are so very powerful in your world. You do not know how powerful as yet, but you are waking up to the truth of this.

As you learned in your last lesson, words are closely linked with beliefs, which in turn program the mind to expect certain results.

I am always amazed how greatly people in your culture are trained to disrespect themselves — trained to put themselves down, trained to discuss many negative issues (which, for the life of me, I can't imagine why), and trained to take no action and stagnate.

Many of you now are feeling restless; this is quite an awakening from your conditioning. You are to be congratulated. You are going in the right direction!

You may have heard that the words "should" and "try" have no place in your vocabulary. This is so accurate! "Should" implies *judging yourself against a standard that has nothing to do with you.*

For example, I've heard people say, "Now that I'm 40, I *should* be further along that I am," or "Because I went to school for so many years, I *should* be making more money," or "I really *should* be more prudent in new relationships."

Why do you judge yourselves so, and why do you listen to your society's judgments? I know you are surrounded by a world in which advertising has supplied many role models that have become key reference points in your culture. How many men and women feel inferior to the imposed standards of a fashion model, a definition of success, or the ability to perform a certain number of tasks within a day?

Stop judging yourselves! You are wonderful as you are! And you are in a culture that constantly transmits distorted information about beauty and love — but more on that later.

Please eliminate the word "should" from your vocabulary. Equally, nix the word "try." That word keeps you motionless. For example, if someone says, "I'm *trying* to learn French," or "I'm *trying* to save money," those words convey that the person is not *learning* or *saving*, but merely *trying* (unsucessfully). "I'm trying to put this function together." "I'm trying to get my sisters to talk to each other." Why not simply say, "I'm putting together a wonderful function," or "I'm getting my sisters to talk to each other — really talk — and they've never done that before! It's so wonderful to be a part of that!" In short, rather than put yourself down and judge yourself against some silly and worthless standard (which was the invention of marketing people to make you feel inferior so that you would seek a solution outside of yourself — with their product, of course!), express the wonderful contributions you make on a daily basis! You don't need to win the Nobel peace prize to be celebrated. And your taking action in this new way will create so many positive results — not just for you, but for everyone. You will actually be sending out a more positive, higher energy!

You can "make a difference" every moment of every day, AND YOU DO!

Another word that falls into this category is "just." "I'm *just* an assistant." "I'm *just* 20 years old." "I'm *just* learning my new job." "Just" is an apology that holds you back from your truth and does not allow you to focus in the moment on what you *are*.

And, please — I could go on for hours about the word "can't"! Understand you are limitless. Understand you *can* do anything! So, PLEASE delete this word immediately!

There are so many words in your language that keep you from realizing your true potential and power. You are all SO powerful — and the only way you could be controlled is to make you think you are powerless. God forbid a number of you "wake up" at the same time — you couldn't be controlled and the structure of power would shift! Guess what? That's exactly what's happening now. Welcome to the club. And things are going to get a lot more fun!

So start by being aware of your language and the language of those you encounter throughout your day.

As with many situations, it will be easier to see the word patterns and effects in those around you at first, but once you become aware of the EXTENT these "power zappers" are infused into your language, you'll start to see them everywhere — even in your own vocabulary.

Homework:

1. In your journal, note the words you hear on a daily basis (from family members, co-workers, friends, strangers, TV, and movie characters) which you think limit that person's power.

Be as specific as possible. For example, have a column entitled "Word" (that you heard) and across from it a column entitled "Hidden Message." Be specific about ALL the ways that word has limited that particular person's belief in himself/herself. The more detailed and the more specific you are, the more powerful this exercise will be for you.

2. In your journal, note the words that you start to hear in your own vocabulary. How do they limit you from your true limitless self? Again, the more detailed you are in exploring the hidden messages you are conveying, the more benefit to you.

3. List all the ways you celebrate yourself in your conversations and thoughts. Again, be specific as to the words you now use, and how using them makes you feel. And then write down how you feel the *next* time you celebrate yourself!

You are all making such great progress. I can hear the wheels in your brains turning from here! You all make me smile. But for now, class dismissed.

"To have knowledge is about 10% of the pie.

To be able to communicate that knowledge effectively

is the other 90% of the pie."

———•◆•———

Lesson 6

I didn't hear you.

As you learned in your last lesson, words are very powerful. They are truly programming keys. As they are such, it will be necessary for you to learn to say EXACTLY what you mean.

In your culture, this will be quite a challenge. There are so many veiled comments, innuendoes, and hidden messages in daily life. Nearly no one says what they really mean, and then you all spend vast amounts of time guessing what this person meant and what that person was thinking. This takes a tremendous amount of energy, does it not?

As you are speaking, become aware of exactly what you wish to say. Although it may be clear to you, is it clear to someone who does not have your point of reference?

How many times have you been in a conversation with a person and you each thought you were talking about an entirely different subject? This actually happens quite frequently, as both parties are relying on their own points of reference — their own "internal library," so to speak.

I once heard a conversation between two people discussing a "short, balding man" and each party was thinking about a different person! It would have been easier to refer to the person by name and not by characteristics that are not uniquely his!

One way to train your mind to communicate more accurately is to imagine that you are talking to a four-year-old. There is little you can "imply" to someone of that age. You make your points simply and clearly, and wait to see if that little person is following your conversation. Please extend the same courtesy to adults, whose minds are cluttered with all the millions of messages accosting them on a daily basis!

You are all on input overload! You are truly being bombarded with messages from every direction — literally. To maintain some semblance of order, your brains filter out as much of the information which you deem "unnecessary" as possible; you then operate with a core of information which is the most needed. *Understand that everyone has a different core of "necessary" information.*

The more you become aware of this, the clearer your communications will become — and the more *effective* you will be in communicating your thoughts and ideas.

I know many of you are enjoying the role of "teacher" in helping to share this and other knowledge with your friends. However, it is never enough to have the knowledge — no matter what that knowledge is. To have the knowledge is about 10% of the pie. To be able to communicate that knowledge effectively is the other 90% of the pie.

How many of you had classes in grade school, high school, or college, where you had no idea what your teacher was saying? Did you ever dread taking a test because you just didn't "get" the material? Some of you had trouble with algebra, some with a foreign language, some with science, and so on. Your teachers all were very intelligent and knew the material well. That does not mean they knew how to teach the information, especially to someone with a totally different point of reference.

So please be aware of the words you choose to communicate your ideas.

The second part of this lesson is to know the times when it is best to discount another's words altogether (perhaps another's actions, as well), and to focus on the intent behind the actions or words.

As you become clearer in your communication and aware of the disparities in your former thoughts and words, you'll be able to see the disparity in others' words as well. Be patient and forgiving.

In your culture, people are rarely appreciated for their intent. This is due largely to the fact that you live in a culture of judgment.

Whether someone makes a comment which you feel is uncalled for, or someone gives you a gift for which you have no place in your life, understand that person is coming from a different point of reference. Rather than focusing on the words or actions, look behind them. You need to adjust your frequency to meet that other person's intent to be able to clearly understand the conversation. If any of you are computer fans, you know that your modems do this when they initially make a connection. They keep adjusting to each other until they are communicating at the same frequency. Then communications can proceed. Computers are fine teachers.

Begin to listen to the *intent* of others' words. This will be most challenging when dealing with those who are closest to you in your life. Open your heart to open your communications. You will actually start to communicate differently, and others will start to notice this difference. You will enjoy this.

This will prepare you for your role of "teacher."

Homework:

In your journal, note what you *intended* to say and what you actually said. Be objective. Try to "hear" your words as someone who does not know you might hear them. Then re-frame your words to make them easier for another to understand. Be precise and list all the incidents where you became aware that someone COULD interpret your words another way. Do this for a minimum of two weeks, preferably for a month. List conversations with your family, your friends, your co-workers, service people, etc.

Keep an ongoing list of conversations where you begin to hear the intent behind the words. Again, be as detailed as possible. In one column, write the words as spoken. Then, in another column, write what you believe the intent to be. Also include whether you confirmed the intent with the other person.

"In the entire universe,

there has never been a

'wrong' decision made."

———◆———

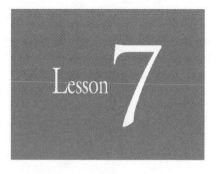

Lesson 7

You're right on schedule.

My dear friends. I know that, living in a world that is driven by schedules, deadlines, appointments that must be kept, and rush hour traffic, you may often feel as though you are rushing through your day to accomplish simple tasks and that there is never enough time in the day to do all the things you wish.

Rush, rush, rush! You've been trained since infancy that this is a "hurry-up" world. Add to these feelings of never having enough time that you also feel as though you should be further along in your life and accomplishments, or further along in reaching your final "goal," and you feel even more pressure to "hurry." Some of you feel you should be "waking up" faster; you feel that you are on the brink of major changes in your life, that you want to break free, but you don't know where to go to, just yet.

It *is* uncomfortable when you begin to disengage from your life's programming. You are all doing some major gear-shifting right now. The entire planet is. And, as your culture has been one of the most materialistic, you will be feeling the greatest effects of this shift. You are seeing through many of the illusions — and believe me, there is much more to come! You are all learning so fast!

Understand that there has NEVER been a time in history like this one. Understand that you are all growing and changing faster than any people have ever had to before! This can create tremendous stress at times.

So, coming from this "rush, rush" conditioning, you now find yourself in this escalating time. You will feel everything "speed up" increasingly as time goes on.

This is why it is imperative for you to SLOW DOWN!

Slow down and relax! You are right on schedule. You are exactly where you are supposed to be right at this moment. You are doing exactly what you are to be doing at this moment! Applaud yourselves for this!

Many of you have not had many people in your life who truly appreciated all the unique facets of what makes you "you"! You may be accustomed to having your faults brought to your attention, but perhaps not your wonderful, unique qualities.

If you have not had many "cheerleaders" on your team, it is time for you to be your own. It is time for you to recognize that you are perfect, right where you are. Drop the comparisons to other people's expectations.

Can you honestly look in the mirror and say, "I am perfect!"? Because THIS is the truth! Once you bring this truth into your consciousness, your entire perspective will change. Then you will see the changes manifest in your life.

If you are already living this truth, you know how powerful a breakthrough this is!

When you believe you are perfect, you relate to others differently. You present yourself as your divine being. And, as a divine being, you see through the illusions of daily, manipulative conditioning. You do not need to fear anything another person could say or do, because you are above that. You do not need to become defensive because one usually feels the need to defend that which is limited, and your perfection has no limits.

Understand that by the word "perfect," I do not mean to imply that you don't make any mistakes. Believe me, we

ALL make what you would call mistakes. We have a different perspective on this.

So, *you* make a mistake; *I* create a learning opportunity that will propel me to a higher level of awareness. Frankly, I like my perspective much better!

You see, in truth there is no "wrong." "Wrong" is fear-based judgment. Many of you have been in periods of stagnation because you were afraid of making a "wrong" decision. At the risk of sounding disrespectful, nothing could be more humorous to me. You see, there is no such thing as a wrong decision. It simply cannot be. In the entire universe, there has never been a "wrong" decision made. This is not to say that someone else might arrive at a different decision, given the same information. *All decisions are perfect for that person, at that time!*

The fact that someone else would have done something differently than you did, or even that *you* would do something differently now than you did before, means nothing. Understand that this is programming to prevent you from realizing your true perfection!!!

How many of you have spent hours berating yourselves through the years over what you judged to be "stupid" decisions and actions? PLEASE STOP THIS RIGHT NOW! All your decisions and actions to this very moment have been absolutely perfect! This is truth!

Just because you may not have your entire life's overview at this moment, you may not be able to see the sequence of events that are unfolding. Truly, there is a plan for your life. Trust that this exists. *Your life is unfolding perfectly, and you're right on schedule.*

When you believe this to be true, you tap into your limitless power, and that can be threatening to those who wish to control you, you understand?

You are wonderful, perfect, limitless, powerful beings. So act like it!

Homework:

1. Make a list of the "stupid" decisions and actions you have made throughout your life. List the events that led up to those decisions and all the reasons why you arrived at the conclusions you did. Please be as detailed as possible. If you get any insights from doing this, write them down, too.

2. Make a list of all the ways in which you are a perfect being. (If this is difficult for you, picture the people in your life who would speak at your funeral, all the different people who may know a different side of you, and all the things they would say about you.)

3. Make a little sign that says "I am perfect" and tape it to your mirror — or to a more private place, if you desire, but where you will see it every day. Get used to saying the words. *When you can say the words and mean them, you will feel the shift in your perception.*

4. Forgive yourself for being hard and judgmental about past actions and decisions. Declare that from now on, you will be supportive of all your choices — no matter what.

Take the time to do all the above steps. There is no deadline.

"If anyone says 'you'd better act <u>now</u>,'

run the other way!"

———◆———

Lesson 8

Who loves you, baby?

The more you disengage from your society's programming, the more you will be able to see the schism between love and fear. Or — more appropriately — between love-based realities and fear-based realities.

As we have talked about your society being mainly occupied with fear-based realities, hopefully you are beginning to see this to be true.

In the course of a day, listen to all the messages you receive that are fear-based. Your television, your radio, your entertainment, your daily personal encounters are so infused with messages of fear: ... the stock market, the economy, new health threats, violence in your streets, "this food has been found to cause cancer," "don't trust members of this government party," drive-by shootings in your neighborhoods and on your freeways, robberies, rapes, child molestation, job layoffs, etc., etc., etc. ... .

The underlying message is "YOU'D BETTER WATCH OUT! THINGS ARE GOING TO GET EVEN WORSE!" You'd better have insurance, vitamins, pills, major medical coverage, weapons, theft deterrents, alarms, and a vote for the correct political candidate!

Your lives are so complicated! From every direction throughout the day, you are being infused with "WHAT IF ... ?" "You'd better be careful ... ," "You're pretty lucky now, but ... ," and "Bad times are on the horizon ... ."

Understand that ALL of these messages are programming for you to be sucked into fear-based realities. And this conditioning is so strong, because it had its beginning when you were babies. However, then you were taught to "watch out" and "be careful" out of love and concern. And because this is how you were first taught to relate to the world, it becomes easy for you as an adult to accept the words and concepts easily and without question. Do you see how brilliantly you are being manipulated? How your child-like trust is being abused?

Understand that when you live in fear, you are not living in your strength and power. In fact, when you live in fear, you aren't even aware that you are powerful. In fact, through the ages, you've all been told that you are poor, pitiful, *powerless* creatures who should be grateful for every crust of bread thrown your way.

"Isn't that awful?" "That poor girl!" "What a pity!" "Be thankful you have a job!" ... I could go on for hours. In your daily routine, you receive literally hundreds of messages sent to separate you from your power and instill fear.

And fear is the number one cause of stress. Fear of losing your job makes you work yourself into a frenzy and not enjoy your career. Fear of financial problems keeps many of you awake at night. Fear of not being loved causes you to do some strange things to get attention.

Well, I'm here to tell you that fear is the biggest illusion. Fear (in most cases) is unnatural. Do you know you only have two instinctive fears? Only two: the fear of falling, and the fear of loud noises. All your other fears are learned — or, more appropriately, conditioned.

You are, in a sense, brainwashed by your culture. Duped by your society. Think of it. You receive messages constantly that keep you in an agitated state of fear. You eat food that has been over-processed and hence do not take in any natural essences and their "teaching" abilities. You override your body's signals for attention with pain killers and drugs. The air you breathe and the water you drink is not clean. In short, you treat your rats in a laboratory better than this, do you not? Awaken and learn how controlled you've been "kept"!

So, how do you reverse the brainwashing procedure? How do you know if someone truly has your best interest at heart or if someone wants to control you?

The answer is really simple. Is the other person/organization coming from a place of love, or a place of fear? Are they telling you that if you don't buy this car today, it won't be here tomorrow, so you'd better act now?

If anyone says "you'd better act <u>now</u>," run the other way! Any time you are being forced to make a decision, this is not in your best interest.

You need to process information in your own way, and *in your own time frame.* You need to read your body's signals and listen to your guidance.

First of all, why is anyone telling YOU what to do? You are the only one who knows what is best for you. You are wise and wonderful. You have so much knowledge; however, you haven't been told you are so knowledgeable.

And secondly, applaud yourselves for being such "good sports," for trusting in those "above" you, in positions of authority. But enough is enough.

Anytime something doesn't feel right, or you feel you are being pressured or are on the receiving end of a fear tactic, simply say, "That doesn't work for me," and remove your-self from the situation.

The more you begin to do this, the more you will see other people reacting to you. You are exercising your true power and other people will respond accordingly. How-ever, know that those with the most to lose from you tapping in to your own power will be the most vocal. This part gets quite fun, actually. And very entertaining! So, stand your ground and grab some popcorn! Just watch the show and enjoy yourself!

And, thirdly, learn what is love and what is fear disguised as love. The word "love" has been so misused in your culture, that it's been used (and *is* used) for many situa-tions and feelings that have nothing to do with love. This will be more difficult for some of you to discern. There are many "love masqueraders" out there. You may have been in a family or a relationship with one (or more) along the way: those who say they are doing something for you "because they love you," when they really only want to manipulate you and control you.

There are many people walking around saying they love this or love that who do not understand the meaning of the word. There are people who may say they love you who do not first love themselves. This is impossible. Until they can fully accept and love themselves, they cannot love another.

So, how do you tell if people love themselves? Well, how do they treat themselves? How do they talk to themselves? Are they loving and accepting of themselves when they make a mistake, or are they critical and shaming? Another way to know is if they need to tell you how much they love themselves. *Be wary of anyone who feels the need to explain that which needs no explanation.*

Learn to discern the "love masqueraders" from the people who truly operate from a place of love in their heart. And there will be more and more masqueraders as the times get crazier, people who have all the solutions, all the answers, and will let you have them " ... for only $29.95, IF YOU ACT NOW!"

Homework:

1. Make a list of all the fear-based messages you encounter in a week's time. Note what is the source of the message (television, radio, newspaper, conversations, etc.) Note what is the implied action to be taken. Who benefits?

2. Note how fear causes stress in your life. Please be as detailed as possible. How would your life be different without each specific fear?

3. As you begin to disengage from fear-based realities and remove yourself from controlling, fear-based situations, what are other people's reactions? Describe the situation, your actions and all the reactions of others involved. Keep this in a separate section of your journal, as this will be an ongoing part of your development and awareness.

4. If you encounter any "love masqueraders" (either in real life or on television, in movies, etc.), make a note of their words and messages and what you feel their true message is. Be as detailed as possible.

5. Congratulate yourself for surviving in a society based on conditioning — and for having the awareness and

commitment to break through the illusions! You are magnificent! You have my deepest respect.

This important and concentrated lesson will be ongoing. But for now, class dismissed.

"Your day is filled with 'triggers'

and you are not even aware of them."

———◦◆◦———

Lesson 9

Breathe easy.

Undoubtedly, you are seeing the patterns of control and fear-based messages infused into your daily culture, and you are separating yourselves from these patterns. You move quickly!

To further help you disengage from this well-structured conditioning, you will need to be more aware of your breath. Sounds simple, does it not? It is. Because I am not asking you to be aware to the extent that masters and yogis are, those who have the benefit of being apart from your hectic society. I am asking you, however, to be aware of your breath when you start to feel stressed or pressured.

And that can be simple.

Let's say, for example, that you are driving your car (or being transported by another means, if that better suits you) and you are late to meet with someone. Perhaps you can feel yourself begin to be stressed by the situation. You begin to focus totally on the traffic, the car in front of you, etc. In short, your entire universe becomes you, your car, and all the "impediments" that are *keeping you* from arriving on time.

At THAT moment, I want you to become aware of your breath. When you feel stressed, you will notice that you either go into "shallow breathing" (which is short rapid breaths that seem to come from the upper chest), or you are not breathing at all!

Why is this? You are actually accessing your more primal survival skills. When you become stressed, your body automatically goes into an "alert" mode and you are standing ready to make your "fight or flight" decision on an instant's notice. And your "shallow" or "not" breathing allows you to be hyperalert and move quickly. This is an excellent skill to have if you are hunting wild animals with nothing more than a spear. Your life would depend on such skills.

However, once again, it is as though your "auto pilot" reflexes are stuck and we need to return you to your manual controls, to be able to deal with the true situation at hand. In short, you are in a constant "hyperalert" mode, ever vigilant, and your body is pumping adrenaline far too often! You've become "hooked" on your own stress, so to speak! Addicted to drama!

Any of a number of situations may trigger your reactions. It may be that your boss wants to talk to you. It may be when you open this month's credit card bill. It may be when your phone rings at a late hour. It may be any one of a million "triggers" throughout the day. Often, your day is filled with "triggers" and you are not even aware of them.

So the best way you can balance out and return to a truer picture of what you are experiencing is to BREATHE. You've always been told to "take a deep breath" when you need to calm down, but you may not understand why this works and why this is so important. When you take several deep and slow breaths, you are slowing your timing down and removing yourself from that "fight or flight" mode.

But don't get discouraged if things don't change after one or two breaths. Learn what your body needs. If you need to take twenty deep breaths, take twenty. If you need to breathe deeply for five minutes, then do that! And if you happen to be able to meditate for a time, so much the better!

You are, in short, getting back in touch with your own wisdom and honoring your body's initial signals of stress. And your body will appreciate your responding to its messages!

I am always amazed to see some of you taking better care of your cars than your bodies! If your car rattles or "sounds funny," it's in the shop the next day. But when your body sends you signals crying out for the same attention, you cover up the messages with pain killers, camouflage its cries with drugs.

So, in essence, it is easier and less expensive to take a few deep breaths than to take pills, is it not? (And much more convenient!)

Simple enough? So get fast, total relief the natural way ... with breath! (And it's free!)

Homework:

1. Over the next several weeks, note in your journal what situations you were aware of that caused you to feel stress. How long did it take your body to get your attention? How were you breathing?

2. Note how long you altered your breathing to get your desired results.

3. How did your perspective change once you were able to return your breathing to "normal"?

4. With each subsequent example of stress, were you able to become aware of the situation more quickly? How did you react to different types of stress?

Your ongoing notes on this will help you to "rise above" the increasing level of stress in your daily life!

Bravo!

"You know how different fuels

affect your car's performance, do you not?

Fuel has an even greater effect on your body."

———◦◆◦———

Lesson 10

Garbage in, garbage out.

I am pleased that you are learning so quickly how to detach from your manipulative societal programming and to feel what "rings true" in your lives.

In addition to observing the outside forces whose effect is to instill fear, you also need to be aware of the "outside forces" that become, in short, "inside forces."

Let's talk about your food. Despite the fact that your culture eats more processed (and manipulated) foods than any other culture on your planet, you are told that your culture is the best on the globe, that few go hungry, that you have plenty. Plenty of <u>what</u>, I might ask?

First of all, let's address how your culture consumes more meat than any other on the globe. You are actually addicted to meat. And more importantly, actually addicted to what is IN the meat. I'm not here to criticize your carnivorous habits, but I am here to inform you how they take their toll on your awareness.

As you already know, your meat is pumped full of hormones, steroids, preservatives, and chemicals so it will "appear" to be more appealing. However, this is not the worst of concerns. Your animals are kept alive in horrid conditions and are finally killed in a factory setting. Needless to say, the creatures know what's coming. Their fear of death becomes all-consuming and their stress levels and hormonal (especially adrenal) secretions are at an all-time high when they pass over.

Understand that this intense state of fear permeates the meat they leave as their legacy. So the "information" you receive from eating your supermarket meat is of "being trapped" and "in a heightened state of fear."

You've heard the adage, "You are what you eat," have you not? Well, guess what? YOU ARE. So, the very foods you eat keep you in a spiral of fear and dependence.

Think of how your society has conditioned you to feel you are "going without" if you do not ingest a large hunk of meat at most of your meals, that you won't be healthy and you won't feel right if you don't. Well, most cultures on the planet don't eat the quantities of meat you do and most are healthier and feel better than you do! Your bodies don't NEED to eat big slabs of meat at every dinner.

And it's even humorous that while so many people have heart disease and cholesterol problems, your society is still advising you to eat LEAN meats, instead of greatly reducing the actual quantity of meat in your diet.

In short, you are being programmed through what you eat! And YOU are the one who chooses what you eat! Isn't this an amazing kind of programming? Your lives do resemble the lives of cattle in a way, do you see? You are being led to the food trough, although you call it a super-market.

I am not saying that you all need to wake up tomorrow and be vegetarians, but I am saying that you need to be conscious about what you put into your body. You know how different fuels affect your car's performance, do you not? Fuel has an even greater effect on your body.

There are many alternatives to your "programmed" food. If you wish to consume meats, consider contacting a health food market or kosher foods store. ASK QUES-TIONS about how the meat has been prepared. Ask how it was raised and how it was butchered. This will give an indication of the level of fear that may be carried in the meat. If you are buying fish, ask where it was caught and when. How fresh is it — how clean are the waters it lives in. You need to know this!

All your strides forward toward becoming more aware and healthy in these intense times could be undermined by your remaining conditioned by the food that you eat.

Know that in more "primitive" times, you ate many things: plants, berries, fruits, barks, roots, greens, nuts, ground-based proteins, fish, fowl, and — occasionally — meat. All your food was fresh and alive, in that you ingested the food's "intelligence."

Your Native Americans understand this. They believed that a plant or animal's "give away" meant the substance now was transformed to a higher vibration, a more advanced form of life. In short, the plant or animal continued living, in a way, in the person who ate it. In short, eating was a spiritual act, an act of love of one species for another.

Plants and animals DO have great intelligence — in their natural forms. However, processed foods have the knowledge processed OUT. Freeze-dried, flash frozen, powdered, reconstituted, dehydrated … I could go on and on!

Add to this that many of you eat "on the run." You do not savor the act of eating. Grab a burger here, a sandwich there. STOP! A mealtime can truly be a wonderful experience to share with people you love when you make time to consider what you are actually doing, not just reacting as you've been conditioned to do.

So be aware of what you do to your body every day. Consider altering your eating habits and patterns. You will see a new clarity in your thoughts, not to mention your skin and eyes! You will come alive!

And you will have a new perspective with much less fear!

Your making these changes will move you forward much faster. And you will be a wonderful example to those around you!

Homework:

1. Note in your journal all the messages you read and hear about food, about what is good, why you should buy it, and what is "on sale" (a pressure situation). How many food messages do you hear in an average day?

2. Keep an ongoing list of what you eat every day. List everything you eat throughout the day. Across from each item you eat, note how you feel, how you react to situations and stress.

If you choose to change your eating habits, know that there will be a period of transition that your body will go through. You may not begin to feel the full effects of your changes for a few weeks. And don't forget to drink lots of PURE water throughout the day!

3. As you change your eating habits, what are other people's reactions? If you encounter negative reactions, ask that person why they feel that way. Note this in your journal.

Thank you all for your dedication and your awareness! I am proud to have such wonderful students!

"If you ever feel as though you are a victim,

it is a gentle reminder that

there is action you need to take."

———⊷◆⊶———

Lesson 11

No victims, please!

Now that you are tapping into your true power and disengaging from your society's programming, you are beginning to see what a marvelous creature you are! Strong, beautiful, wise, and wonderful! And the more you tap into your power, the more "magical" your life will appear to be. And not to mention, fun!

Therefore, the lesson for today is a big one. It is one that has been labeled "victim mentality" in your society.

Know that "victim mentality" is the direct result of your societal conditioning. It truly separates you from your power. The more you feel like a victim, the less likely you are to pose a threat to those in supposed power.

What is victim mentality? It's the "Poor Me!" attitude, the "I'm so poor," "I hate my job," "Times are tough," or "Nobody loves me" attitude. It's the "Feel sorry for me because I'm alone," or "Feel sorry for me because I have it tougher than you do" attitude. It's the "Can you believe this is the fourth time someone has dumped me in six months!" attitude.

Please! Listen to these messages! These are not the messages of wise and limitless beings! These are the mantras of conditioned little hamsters!

First of all, anytime you are feeling like a "victim" or that someone or something has just "done something to you," you are missing the point. Remember: 1) all things are happening just as they should and you're right on schedule, and 2) if you ever feel as though you are a victim, *it is a gentle reminder that there is action you need to take!* That's it! The universe is not trying to make your life miserable because you're a good person!

Any time you complain to another, you are taking useful energy that could be used for action, and not only wasting it on useless conversation, but actually strengthening the "problem." What you focus your attention on will actually become stronger.

Do you know anyone who spends all their time complaining that they do not have enough money? The situation probably compounds itself, does it not? They are actually creating a bigger problem with their complaining and giving energy to the situation, instead of finding a solution while it is still a small concern.

Situations will get your attention, just as dis-eases will with your body. They will start out as a minor irritation to get your attention. If you address the situation immediately, there is no need for it to escalate.

Do you know anyone who always has a calamity? Always has a series of crises to address? Not only is this person needing stronger "hints" to get their attention, but they probably love the drama of it all. This is totally unnecessary!

When you are in tune with your power, your guidance, and you are centered, you will receive all the information you need. And when you receive the information you need, you will be able to act on it as soon as a situation comes to your attention! You will not need that "2 x 4" that you may have needed in the past! This is one of the many benefits of becoming more aware of who you truly are!

Believe me, I am not saying this is going to be easy. Your entire culture is designed to foster and support feelings of victimization. All the messages you receive throughout the day reinforce this. So this is the time to claim your power and your true identity!

So I am asking all of you to become "Victim Busters"! Although you cannot bust someone else's victim mentality, you can certainly address your own.

Know that when you start to feel victimized by the world, your boss, your family, your parents, etc., you have the opportunity to nip this situation in the bud! First of all, CONGRATULATE YOURSELF for being aware enough to recognize this!

Then ask yourself, "What action do I need to be taking?" Or, in your meditations, ask your guidance for a direction of needed action. And ask to be *ready* to receive the information. Many times, victim mentality is another form of denial.

Denial? In other words, say for example, a man constantly complains that his job is so terrible. Well, why is he there? Because the economy is so bad, or because he should be happy he has a job — any job???!!! Please! He is probably in that situation because he isn't happy in that job; he doesn't have the confidence to try what would truly make him happy, *so he justifies his present situation by creating a victim scenario! It is not cause and effect; it is effect, then cause!*

Perhaps this man needs to connect with his power and identity to truly learn he is wonderful and limitless, to celebrate his unique self, to truly love and appreciate himself. THEN he will learn what work would bring him joy. THEN he will need to take action to accomplish his goal of a joyful career. And this will come from a place of self-love and appreciation, of limitless hope and courage and strength.

Or the man/woman who complains about having been "dumped" four times in six months! Well, what action needs to be taken here? We could go on for hours! But I think you see the point. Anytime you feel you must "settle" for something, you are in a victim mentality.

In short, when you begin to feel like a victim, smile at the opportunity you have to make a shift forward to more power and joy and, after a while, this awareness will become "second nature," as you awaken to your total magnificence!

Homework:

1. Tune in to all the victim messages you encounter throughout the day. Your advertising is full of them! Getting you to feel a victim and separated from your power and magnificence has sold many products and services! List all the messages you hear in a week's time: from the media, from conversations, and from your own thoughts!

2. Note when you start to feel like a victim. Firstly, congratulate yourself for being so aware!!! Write down what the situation is all about. Next, list what actions you feel you could take to address the concern. Also note how you may have reacted to this situation before.

The more you practice "Victim Busting," the faster you will progress in your increasing awareness! You will also subtly show others that there is another way to look at a situation!

Bravo!

"Anyone who focuses on being 'in control'

is, in short, focusing on death ...

of their awareness, anyway."

———◆———

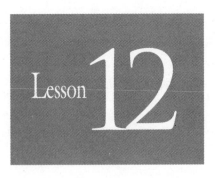

Lesson 12

Mid-term Exam: Change and Control

As you are progressing in your lessons, I want to let you know of a few "measuring sticks" along the way.

Perhaps, as a child, your parents measured your height upon a wall, and you were able to see your growth from year to year. As you are growing even more rapidly in your awareness than you have ever experienced before, I want to give you the tools to measure your own growth. Let's talk about control.

There are so many people in your culture — well educated, intelligent, accomplished people — who feel lost when they sense they are "out of control." Let's take a look at this.

Why are so many people addicted to control? Because they are fear-based and they feel that if they are "in control" that nothing can harm them, that there will be no surprises that will strike them unaware.

Please! Talk about illusions!

Understand that control is a big illusion. You cannot control anything (although you can *influence* many things). You are in a wonderful dance of energy that moves and transforms constantly. To control this undulating essence would be to cease to be alive. In short, anyone who focuses on being "in control" is, in short, focusing on death … of their awareness, anyway.

If you find yourself in a situation where you are attempting to control it or people, STOP. This will be a "mid-term," so to speak, a chance to put all your lessons to date to the test.

Stop. Breathe. Remember that you are right on schedule and right where you are to be at this moment.

Take time to get grounded. (Meditate if possible, even for a short time). Are you acting out of love, or are you acting out of fear? Why do you feel the *need* to control? Is this a habit, or can you identify what is motivating you?

Wanting to be "in control" may surface in situations that are not so familiar: when you meet new people, when you are outside your comfort zone. Perhaps a job interview. Perhaps a first date. Perhaps meeting a friend's parents. Giving a speech. Meeting with the IRS. Buying a car or a home. Dealing with the bank.

Wanting to be "in control" is not the manner of someone who knows their true power and magnificence. Knowing this is so is another reminder that you are becoming aware in new ways and disconnecting from old programming. How wonderful! Also know that this behavior no longer serves you. It is, indeed, holding you back from growing at a rapid rate.

So learn to appreciate this "test" and you will score well!

Likewise, those who say they hate change. In short, people do not "hate" change, they *fear* change.
This is, of course, tied in to wanting to control.

Know that change means growth. Change *is* growth, and you will not be asked to change or grow at a rate faster than you can handle. This would be impossible. Because as you grow and change, you are being prepared for the next step, the next "change." And to shy away from change — or to refuse change — is being ungrateful for the wonderful new learning you will acquire, the gift of growth.

Although neither change nor control is negative, your perception of these go back to comparing them to what you think should be happening, to how you think things SHOULD be. Abandon these thoughts.

As you are moving ahead at precisely the correct rate, *welcome all the change that comes into your life. All change is a gift for more learning and wonderful development.* And if you don't see all the reasons why at the moment, don't berate yourself. Understand you will know the entire picture when it is the perfect time. Until then, trust that you are right on track, because YOU ARE.

You are changing into a wonderful, loving, powerful creature who does not need the illusion of control to be powerful.

Trust this is so. It will truly be revealed to you when it's time.

"You have been programmed to believe that

the only action you can take is to complain,

and that by complaining, you are taking action."

———•◆•———

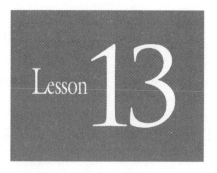

Lesson 13

Complain, complain, complain!

I trust that these lessons are starting to build on each other. The teachings overlap in many ways.

So, this lesson is about a pattern that needs to be dissolved, either within yourselves or — if you already have eliminated this from your repertoire — a pattern that you can be instrumental in dissolving in others.

I'm talking about the complainer. You've been trained to complain. Your entire culture does this.

Your sitcoms are full of complainers ... your political figures, your movies, your news. You are surrounded by complainers. Let's take a look at this.

You have been programmed to believe that the only action you can take is to complain, and that by complaining, you are taking action. Nothing could be more false!

But consider how well this scenario works for those "in control" in your society: your political figures, your corporate chiefs, your religious leaders. If the only action you take is to complain, you are then harmless to them. In addition, by complaining, you are adding energy to whatever the problem is, and actually *compounding* the concern, to have a bigger problem to complain about! Then you feed more energy to that problem and the endless spiral takes you further and further into non-action.

Know that the energy needed to change a situation is *only a fraction* of the energy involved in complaining and worrying about any problem!

Change is quite easy, once you *know* you have the power to change — AND YOU DO!

How many people do you encounter in a week's time who spend their conversations complaining about their jobs, their relationships, their living quarters, other people, the city in which they live, the state of the economy, the latest sports defeat, and so on?

By complaining, you are taking needed energy away from fueling your self-esteem!

When you believe you are a powerful and wise being, you have no need to complain. You see how things are working on a grander scale, and for areas you wish to change, you make your "plan of attack." Most importantly, you feel energized, not drained!

Know that complaining is actually an energy all its own. It is a negative downward spiral that feeds on itself. That is why you may hear someone complain and then others readily join in. It's really no fun to complain alone! *Complaining is commiserating with others about how powerless you are.* Your body then takes on the appearance and the posture of a helpless waif. And when you feel powerless, you are quite lacking in the area of self-esteem, are you not?

How many people do you know who shuffle around and moan and groan about how they hate their job, their marriage, their boss, their in-laws, etc., and they look as though all the energy has been drained out of their bodies? Well, it has! And it is best not to be around that energy. So, if you encounter a complainer, simply say, "When you are ready to take action, you will. Until then, I prefer not to be around wasted energy."

This may not win many friends who are stuck in their victim roles, but you will be doing these people a service by reflecting the truth back to them.

Likewise, agree to take gentle action should you ever be aware of yourself complaining.

Homework:

1. In your journal, note how many different topics you hear people complaining about in a two-week period — the more bizarre and obscure, the better.

2. If you find yourself complaining, note how you feel and describe your body posture. Also note if others join in to make it a "complain party."

3. Note in your journal if you hear yourself complaining. When you become aware of it, simply stop this activity and begin to map out a plan of action. It does not need to be the final plan, but it will set solutions in motion! Note also how your energy shifts by doing this.

4. As an ongoing assignment, note in your journal how you deal with complainers with whom you come in contact. Note their reaction and how you feel about the situation.

You are all moving so quickly! Your help on this issue will be invaluable in "waking up" many people, even though you may not as yet realize this.

"A justification usually begins with

why you support a present situation, or rather

why your EGO supports not making a change!"

———◆———

Lesson 14

Eliminate your need to justify.

This lesson builds on the previous one. As you are now more aware of the intense conditioning and manipulation of your society, you will be prepared to address your need to justify.

Justifying is, in a way, the opposite of complaining. Initially, it sounds as though you are being positive and supportive of a present situation. However, know that in truth, justifying *is* complaining!

When you are living in line with your heart (or, in other words, when you are in balance with your true nature and doing the things that bring you joy), you never think about how others perceive your words or actions, because they are true and from your heart. They are your purest expressions.

However, when actions and words do not come from the heart, this is when your society has a tendency to fall into a pattern of justification. And the need to justify takes a tremendous amount of energy.

So, firstly, what do I mean by "the need to justify"?

If someone is unhappy with their job, they may say something like, " … I'm paid very well, the location is good, and I really don't want to make a career switch and start out on the bottom rung of the ladder in another field … ." Or, "My commute is only 40 minutes. I know many who drive twice as long." Or, "It's really not so bad to be with my friend who only talks about himself/herself. I've finally learned how to tune the conversation out." Or, "My boss is really preoccupied, so he doesn't have any idea he's so abusive."

If someone is unhappy with a relationship, they may say something like, "… It's really not so bad — it's better than being alone! Besides, with AIDS today, I'm pretty lucky I don't have to worry about that."

These are reasons that the ego gives you to JUSTIFY your not taking action that would be in alignment with your heart and true nature. The justification usually begins with *why you support a present situation*, or rather *why your EGO supports not making a change (!)*, why the ego defends the status quo.

Understand what this is really all about. The justifier and the complainer are one and the same, but appear to be opposites! When you take action that is in alignment with your heart and spirit, you are acting from your power. You are expressing your flowing energy, and that can be intimidating to those who would rather control you.

If you are working because you LOVE the work, you do not care what others may say. You are "untouchable" to others' attempted manipulations … the same when you are in a wonderful relationship.

Just as your society has taught you to feel powerless as a single entity, many people want you to believe that justifying your present situation *is all the action you need to take.*

Do you see how, by your justifying not taking action, those "in control" have no reason to concern themselves with you?

You need to know the truth: You are powerful. You are limitless. You deserve to have everything wonderful in life! You deserve to have a career you love, to surround yourself with beauty, to have loving relationships. You can do anything your heart desires when you tune in to your true essence! And *the action that is needed is to find out what you would love to do, or with whom you wish to spend your time, to make you feel alive!*

Homework:

1. Identify the justifying messages you hear on the radio or TV. Write them down in your journal. Become aware of the amount of justification in your media.

2. Note when you hear someone justify in a conversation with you. Are you willing to voice your response as "That sounds like a justification of the situation."? You are not judging the situation or the person by doing this, but simply reminding the person of what they are indeed doing.

3. Become aware of when you justify. Is it a strongly entrenched habit, or an occasional phrase? How do you feel when you become aware of your justifying?

"Next to your close relationships,

no other subject seems to draw up more emotion

in your society

than the subject of money."

———◆———

Lesson 15

Buddy, can you spare a dime?

This lesson is a rather big one. In fact, next to your close relationships, no other subject seems to draw up more emotion in your society than the subject of money.

People *define* themselves by how much money they can accumulate or how they obtain it. Using money as a standard, people restrict themselves in whom they can meet and learn from (if they don't fall into the same class level of money), and people choose many strange options due to this illusion.

I know that your culture is so focused on money. This may be a challenging lesson to learn, so we will structure this one a bit differently. We'll start with the homework:

1. So, what is money? What does it mean to you? (List as many aspects as you can think of.)

2. What emotions come up when you think of money?

3. What emotions come up when you think about *not* having money?

4. What people in your life influenced you about money and why?

5. Complete the sentences:

> "What I love most about money is ..."
>
> "What I like least about money is ..."
>
> "If I had all the money in the world, I'd ..."

Thank you for your participation in this exercise. There is usually much energy tied up in feelings about money ... more than you know.

In short, remember that money is an exchange; a way to interact with other people; a means of contact, or rather, *a means of connecting*. That's it!

However, the *amount* of your exchange is tied closely to your self-image and self-worth, and those are both illusions!

Think of the term, "self-image." The *self* is a projection of your ego; *image* is an illusion. Remember your true essence is a powerful, limitless spirit. Your "projection of illusion," or your "self-image" is nothing more than *a web of limits* you've created. And this web of limits is not real. Perhaps you've seen computer-generated drawings of a human figure where you can see an underlying structure or a meshwork frame. This is, in essence, what your mind creates and presents to you as who you are, how you are defined: *your web of limits!*

Let's say, for example, you "are" a stock broker, or a teacher, or a physician, or whatever. You have probably set up a template of what a stock broker's, teacher's, or physician's life *should* be like: what type of dwelling you should have, what type of vehicle is acceptable, how you should dress, what is acceptable behavior.

How many people choose a career because they desire a certain lifestyle, not because the work brings them joy? This is backwards. And this is why many people are "waking up" to find themselves unmotivated by their jobs, feeling somehow that there must be more, that some elusive element is missing.

These images have nothing to do with your true nature or essence. These are merely projections.

And because they are projections, they can change when you change your beliefs about them, your agreements to accept them as real.

Oftentimes people who make the most money cannot tell you how they do it. They do not concern themselves with making money. That is not their focus.

Look at your "stars." Some of them, who are truly doing what they love, are just "in the flow" and totally in harmony with universal energies. Look at a fine musician, or a dancer, or some of your athletes or performers. They are truly doing what they love to do and the money just flows in.

However, not all of your "stars" are motivated by such pure principles. Many of your "stars" are truly chasing after the money only. These are the people who seem to have very "rocky" careers, tremendous ups and downs. And they focus on money entirely. They worry about money and they feel victimized by money.

Money is an exchange. Money is energy. Be clear in your intent when you deal with money, whether you are buying your weekly groceries or paying your light bill. Acknowledge the exchange and then the universe, for the opportunity of this experience. Look into the eyes of those you experience the exchange with. This is the true energy.

"How many of your parents celebrated

your adolescent transformations,

like the caterpillar to the beautiful butterfly?"

———◆———

Lesson 16

Growing pains

Your conditioning is not just a product of your society. Think of how parents' beliefs create their child's reality.

What the parents believe to be "absolute truths" are instilled into their children as reality: their fears; their prejudices; their anxieties and their frustrations; their concepts of religion and government; what one can expect from life.

Many times, a family with young children may appear to be harmonious and functional, but the truth is that the children are not yet of an age to question these beliefs.

Now look at adolescence. This is a time when children begin to "compare notes," so to speak, with their peers. They discover that their friends are beginning to question their parents' "absolute truths," just as they are. Add to this all the physical changes occurring to the adolescent body, and it is a time of great change.

The more tightly the parents hold on to their belief structure or "absolute truths," the more they will *justify* their reality by discounting their children's challenges as "just the hormones talking."

Many adolescents find their heartfelt questions and yearnings totally dismissed by their parents. This is the cause of the pain and confusion of adolescence: feeling you are insignificant, being told that your emerging truth is totally invalid, that your senses are wrong, and that you are supposed to conform to the status quo.

How many of your parents celebrated your adolescent transformations, like the caterpillar to the beautiful butterfly? How many of you were praised for your queries? How many applauded you for challenging the status quo?

Unfortunately, in your society, those who challenge the status quo are seen as threatening "outlaws" and become outcasts. This rejection then creates the need for stronger peer bonds, a validation of one's inner truth. You see the adolescent's compulsive movement to friendships, sexual relationships, group activity, and gangs, to literally validate what they feel to be true — a different truth from that of their parents.

Many of you remember this pain of adolescence and you have remained silent in your ongoing challenge of the status quo. You've discounted societal and parental programming in secret, and these feelings of pain and isolation continue to the present.

KNOW THAT YOU ARE NOT ALONE! Just because you don't see validation of this "belief busting" in your newspapers or on TV, know that many more than you would think share your thoughts and feelings, and the numbers grow every day!

Do not be afraid to begin to talk about your thoughts and concerns; your doing so will show many others this is acceptable and necessary. But carry with you the strength to combat your new dismissals. You will receive them. They will only be an indication of who is fear-based, and it is best to remove yourself from that energy if there is no request for your teachings.

Homework:

1. What patterns established in adolescence do I carry with me now?

2. How have these patterns changed to adapt to my present life?

3. What situations today (if any) trigger the feeling of adolescent pain?

"Procrastinating takes an

enormous amount of energy."

———⋅◆⋅———

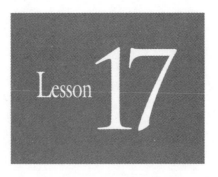

Lesson 17

Wait a minute! Wait a minute!

This lesson deals with a subject that touches all of you at times. I'm talking about procrastination. But this subject is really quite complex, and I would like you to know this topic from "all sides."

Procrastination really involves many of the lessons to date. It combines them all into the appearance of a single act of protest. Let's look closer:

If there is something you are procrastinating against, why is that? Perhaps the task is not in line with your true passions and purpose? Then you are receiving valuable information. Perhaps the task is not necessary at all. You must decide if it is worthy of your attention and energy.

If a simple, yet necessary task has been looming over your head for months and you always find an excuse for not doing it, why not have someone else perform the task for you? Simple enough? Cross it off your check list!

But, you see, this will bring up self-esteem issues (are you "worth" having someone else perform a task for you just because you choose not to do it?), money issues, complaining, and justification issues!

Procrastinating takes an enormous amount of energy. And usually the energy involved in finding other activities to focus on instead greatly outweighs the energy involved in completing the task.

The time has come for you to master your daily tasks and duties, so you may focus on more important, larger issues. So you will need to reduce procrastination in this area.

But another area of procrastination I wish to address at the moment is one that appears as you grow in your personal development. As you grow and change, you will begin to "outgrow" some of your friends and family members. This may feel uncomfortable, at first. You may then experience a period of procrastination in your own growth, so that you may "re-enter" familiar relationships you have outgrown!

Understand that this is quite usual. Growth comes in "tiers." You will experience periods of rapid change, then a period of leveling off and assimilation. Then another period of growth, then a time to assimilate these new changes. During these times of assimilation, you will be tempted to procrastinate and not claim your new "persona" or to find reasons not to continue in your development.

Take a look at your close relationships. Are those closest to you supportive of your growth and exploration, or are they critical and judgmental? If your answer is the latter, you will be very tempted to procrastinate in your development, finding reasons why there are many other tasks that need your attention first.

Be open and honest with yourself during these times. Look inside to learn the reasons why you take certain actions. Love yourself for your choices, whatever they may be, and be proud of all your growth and courage to change. And trust that in being supportive of yourself, you are training others to be supportive of you, too.

Homework:

List any present projects/situations where there may be an element of procrastination.

List the situation/project. List why you are procrastinating and what action you now plan to take.

"Know that your history of feeling like a square peg is invaluable to you now."

———◄◆►———

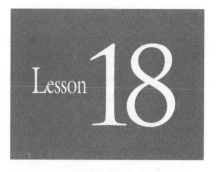

Lesson 18

Square pegs

My dear friends,

I know that many of you have felt as though you have not "fit in" at times in your lives. As this is a pivotal area, we need to address this so that you understand all the reasons for your feelings over many years.

From the time you were small children, your innate wisdom was not in agreement with many things you saw, with many directives on how you were to behave, and more importantly, what you were told you SHOULD want.

This may have been the origin of pain in your childhood and young adulthood for some of you. The more you listened to your inner guidance, the more you were ridiculed or ostracized.

You may have gone through periods of time when you wondered, "What is *wrong* with me that I can't ... ?" (fill in the blanks). "What's wrong with me that I can't get excited about working 9–5, that I choose not to be married, that I'm not interested in what my friends are interested in, that I have different values from my parents, that I look at death differently than this society does?"

So, before we go further, it will be necessary to go back through your life and bring up the events where you felt you didn't fit in.

1. When I was a small child, I didn't feel I fit in because:

2. When I was between the ages of 7–12, I didn't feel I fit in because:

3. During my teen years, I didn't feel I fit in because:

4. As a young adult, I didn't feel I fit in because:

5. I never felt I fit in with certain aspects of my family because:

6. I never felt I fit in with certain aspects of my spouse/relationships because:

7. I never felt I fit in with certain aspects of society because:

Thank you for your work and dedication. Understand that these feelings of not fitting in were a blessing, though I'm sure that's not how it felt. Those closest to you probably were not feeling what you were, and therefore they were uncomfortable with your being different. They may have made you "pay" for their discomfort.

Know that your history of feeling like a "square peg" is invaluable to you now. As times become more chaotic and fear-based, understand that you have a history of tuning out the nonsense and listening to your own wisdom and directions.

Now is the time to shift uncomfortable feelings from the past into a new light. What may have been a cause of pain for many years will be a source of strength for you from this point forward.

Now is the time to learn the truth of your attributes, your strengths, and your wisdom. Look back on your life with gratitude and appreciation. And take time to celebrate the feeling of being a "square peg."

Your trust in yourself will be rewarded at last, and you will begin to see how many "square pegs" there really are — and how you are creating a beautiful new design in which you all will fit perfectly!

"There is no such thing as an unloving person.

But a person who is not in touch with his/her essence

will be further away from the true nature of love."

———◦◦◦———

Lesson 19

Where is love?

This will be a very complex subject. The word "love" has many meanings, innuendoes, and hidden implications in your world. Love is often misunderstood and misused, and many well-intentioned people may have used love to manipulate you — from your family to your friends, to your boss, to your advertisers, to your governments.

So, what is love? Unfortunately, the true meaning of love is a bit elusive in your culture and your language. Think of your understanding of love as the tip of the iceberg, so to speak.

Love is infinite. Love is divine energy, and you are all made of love. This is true. There is no such thing as an unloving person. But perhaps a person who is not in touch with his true essence will be further away from the true nature of love. However, everyone is capable of reconnecting with the infinite power of love.

How many of you have had family situations or relationships where a question was posed to you that if you loved that person enough, then you would do [whatever that person wanted]? It may have been a parent, it may have been a lover, a friend, a child. This is manipulation masquerading as love. Love is without conditions or expectations.

How many times have you heard someone say that if their mate would only do this, then they would truly be able to love them more? I once heard a husband tell his wife that if she lost weight, he would be able to love her more! And listen to your advertising — these messages are bombarding you on a daily basis — that if you buy this car or those clothes, then you will attract the perfect people into your life and you will be complete.

I do not know if you realize how these messages subliminally program your thoughts, expectations, and in effect, your reality!

Let's look at how love with condition and expectation may be a part of your daily life. We'll look at only two of the most common relationships, although you may see the same "symptoms" in your other relationships:

Parent/child relationships

As a parent, you of course want to protect and guide your child, teaching him/her what you know and value, and to give the child the skills and security to develop their own unique expression. However, because much conditioning is passed down from generation to generation, you also may be conditionally giving love to your child to obtain certain desired behaviors. Believe me, I'm not saying child-rearing in these times is easy, but please be clear about how you use love in this important, formative relationship!

Your child must know that you will love them "no matter what" — no matter what they may do, no matter what they may say. You can alter behaviors with other methods, but never imply that if they choose to take a certain action, they will risk losing your love! And even if you feel this is not a concern in your relationship with your child, when was the last time you verbalized this? What you may take for granted as a "given," your child may not.

As an "adult child," you may encounter your parent's manipulative behavior in the present or remember it from the past. As a child, did you feel that you had your parents' love NO MATTER WHAT? — no matter what you did, or what "trouble" you got into? Did you ever worry yourself sick about the thought of doing something that would cause them to abandon you?

Many of you have experienced your parents' divorce or unloving relationship and may be still feeling that somehow that reflects back on you. However, this is not a therapy session; there are many useful options to "work through" feelings you carry from this time. Just be aware whether you feel likely to pass any of these expectations and conditioning on to your children.

Romantic relationships

Know that in your society, it is difficult (if not impossible) to eliminate expectations and conditions from many relationships. Look at marriage; it is based on expectations, is it not? And now that you have "prenuptial agreements," you are defining what to expect from a marriage and what to not expect!

How many marriages do you know of where the partners are truly there for each other's growth, no matter what direction that may take? Probably not too many. If one partner grows in one direction, it may cause the other to feel insecure and abandoned.

But with any romantic relationship, if you enter into a relationship to have another person make you feel complete, you will not have the idyllic life you may expect. You will learn many valuable lessons, yes — but they will probably come with a higher price that you are anticipating.

131

From Lesson Eight, you are now more aware of and able to discern the "love masqueraders" in your life, and to set your boundaries. From this point forward, your ability to love without conditions will re-define what love means for you.

Homework:

1. As a child, were you ever in fear of losing your parent's love? If so, what was the situation that caused this fear?

2. What relationships, if any, have you experienced where you felt love was (to some degree) conditional?

3. If you are a parent, how are you *not* passing along conditional patterns of behavior to your children?

"Many of you who find it difficult to ask for help

are the first to help your friends

when they are in need."

———◆———

Lesson 20

Asking for help

This is another lesson that may be a "breeze" for some of you, and very difficult for others. Those of you who came from critical families and situations from your youth may find this a bit taxing.

As you all continue to feel the constraints of time, energy, support, and life changes, keep in mind that there is a very simple way to not become overwhelmed during these intense times.

How many of you feel comfortable asking for help?

Do you feel as though if you ask for help, you are admitting that you are unable to perform your tasks?

If asking for help is a large lesson for you, I recommend you learn the reasons why that is so. More than ever, it will be imperative to ask for help in the coming months and years.

Please remember, the first objective is for you NOT TO BECOME OVERWHELMED when daily tasks and life changes occur. So you need to have skills at your disposal to move through changes with ease.

I know many of you are "juggling" many items at once — your jobs, your families, your personal growth, and much more — during these "concentrated" times. At any other time in history, this would be quite a feat. But, now, with all the changes that are in motion and with others yet to come, this is incredible. You are all living the life of Superman and perhaps not aware of it, and this "Superman" role has become your culture's norm.

You don't have to be a single mother holding down two jobs to feel the pressure. You are all going through an incredible time! You are to be congratulated for maintaining yourselves so well! (And if you *are* a single mom, you have our deepest respect!)

That's why it is IMPERATIVE to:

1. Take care of yourself:
   Rest, eat well, drink a lot of water.
2. Meditate.
3. Surround yourself with supportive people.
4. Eliminate stressful situations from your life wherever possible.
5. Don't hesitate to ask for help.

Many of you who find it difficult to ask for help are the first ones there to help your friends when they are in need. I am now asking you to be able to receive what you so freely give. People love to help their friends and family members. Helping another gives one a sense of value and purpose. So asking for help actually completes a circle and gives gifts to both the giver and receiver. In asking for help, you are giving a gift to one who can assist you. This truly is a "win/win situation," do you see?

So, the first step here is to become aware of your patterns when you begin to feel overwhelmed, so you can "nip the situation in the bud" and then solicit help from the appropriate person or persons. In order to do this, I would like you to remember a time when you felt overwhelmed, stressed out, "freaked out," or whatever term you use.

Usually, a situation builds over time and there are several "warning signs" that you may choose not to heed. So please complete the following:

1. A time when I felt overwhelmed was:

2. The length of time from when I first felt an "inkling" of irritation to when I was totally overwhelmed was:

3. When you felt overwhelmed, did you ask for help?

4. If so, what were the results?

   If not, why not?

5. The first "warning bell" of the situation was:

6. Had you heeded this "warning bell," what would be different?

(You can apply the same questions to other situations you have encountered, to get the necessary information.)

Those of you who "stress out" over situations that could be easily resolved with help from another person are not only making things much more difficult than they need to be, but ARE MAKING THINGS DIFFICULT BECAUSE YOU CHOOSE THEM TO BE. You are actually *electing* to continue a long-established pattern of stress. Know that this behavior no longer serves you and will drain your valuable energy if you continue.

The more you can bring these situations to your conscious awareness, the more you can alter your behavior.

Understand that in your true identity there are no judgments or expectations. You are powerful and wise. But being powerful does not mean that you must do everything yourself. YOU ARE POWERFUL TO MAKE DECISIONS THAT WILL CREATE A LIFE OF JOY.

It really is that simple — the choice between joy and one of difficulty and feeling overwhelmed.

It's up to you.

"You were taught that work is solely

a physical or mental effort

... toil; labor."

———◆◆———

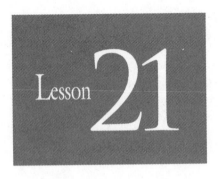

Lesson 21

All work and no play

You are all so hard working and dedicated! But as you may know, there has never been a time like this when everyone is working so hard, working at things that perhaps do not bring you true joy. You may feel you have to work so long and hard in order to have a few moments of joy.

You work all year long and then perhaps take a short vacation. Some of you even spend your vacation working in some manner.

Work! Work! Work!

You've been all taught that work is a privilege. Work proves you are not lazy. Work contributes to the greatness of the whole collective. Well, let's take a look at the word, "work."

Your dictionary states work is "1. Physical or mental effort or activity directed toward the production or accomplishment of something; toil; labor."

Toil. Labor. Physical or mental effort ... ! Do you see the point?

Work is totally based in the material: *physical* or *mental* effort. There is nothing about the spiritual aspect, the flow from somewhere higher.

As we stated earlier, when people are engaged in "work" they love doing, we are not talking about physical OR mental effort. We are talking about being one with your innate wisdom, your essence. Then you are involved in a joyous process.

But the more you are taught that work is solely a physical or mental effort — toil, labor — then you are masses easily controlled.

Think of many corporations. The people who run large companies may be doing so out of love for the process. But few in subordinate positions share in this energy. Or some people "at the top" are so out of touch with what truly brings them joy that they have bargained for what gratifies their ego: the money, the illusion of power, the prestige, the material comforts.

This is one reason corporate America is breaking down. The "work force" doesn't buy the company line anymore. The workers are more in touch with their essence than many "above" them.

Companies that work well and generate profit are those in which everyone shares in the energy of effortless contribution — companies where each individual's essence and creativity is valued, where there is a common goal that unites the entire work force. And a sense of pride follows, as a result.

As we are reaching an end to this "work" cycle (or collective mindset about what work is to be), many of you are feeling uncomfortable with your line of work. Many of you feel frustrated, but may not as yet know where to go next.

Ask yourself how you truly feel about your present work. Does it bring you a sense of joy and of contribution, or do you regard your job as an obligation?

Understand all will unfold at the proper time. Until then, take a break — you're already working too hard!
(So, no homework for this lesson!)

"If a recurring situation is becoming a nuisance,

you are actually creating it as a way

to move through it

and achieve a 'giant step' forward in your growth."

———⟵◆⟶———

Lesson 22

Thanks, but "No thanks!"

This lesson is about your most common elements of stress, those which translate to the important lessons that will propel you forward in your growth.

Oftentimes, you will be confronted with situations that may seem unpleasant and awkward. Similar situations may occur over and over again. You may discuss this situation with your friends and tell them how tired you are becoming of having to deal with this situation — AGAIN.

In essence, many situations are created for you to gain the awareness to say, "That doesn't work for me," but until you arrive at that point of knowing, you may go through a series of conditioned reactions that have become quite an entrenched pattern in your behavior.

If a recurring situation is becoming a nuisance, you are actually creating it as a way to move through it and achieve a "giant step" forward in your growth. However, at the time, you only feel the discomfort and wish you can find a quick solution. Oftentimes, I hear people say, "I just wish this (situation) were over!"

The situation may involve an abusive relationship, an unappreciative boss, a domineering family member, a pushy salesperson. These are all opportunities to find out exactly WHAT makes you feel awkward, why it does that, and to take action. And once you do so, everything will change.

You are disengaging from a society that has told you that you have little power, and are moving toward the realization that you are incredibly powerful. Then, when you realize how powerful you truly are, you can take effective action. This will move you forward very quickly, because you are not only changing behavioral patterns, but you are also changing your view of yourself — in essence, your identity.

Claiming your power is often misunderstood as being assertive or aggressive. Power is not a loud voice or a dramatic exit. Power is not force or brawn. These are only illusions. Power is a different kind of strength altogether. Your society is full of violent people who have no idea what their unique strengths are. So, instead of drawing on their power, they use external forms or weapons (like guns) to feel the ILLUSION of power. However, when these people are not carrying guns, they feel insignificant.

A truly powerful person is loving and compassionate.

You can claim your power in your own, unique way. Each person has their own strengths. Some people cannot be intimidated; some are quick-witted; some are very charming; some very sweet and sincere; some have a wonderful sense of humor; some always see "the silver lining." Being powerful does not necessarily mean you must beat your fist on the conference table. It means owning your unique strengths and projecting them, whatever they may be, finding your own way to say, "That doesn't work for me."

Once you do, you will see your world change, your growth accelerate, and those around you will respect you as a powerful person.

Homework:

1. Make a list of people you've been led to believe are powerful. List their qualities and why they are not truly powerful.

2. Make a list of people you feel ARE truly powerful. Why do you consider them powerful and what are their unique qualities?

3. Make a list of your strengths, or your "good qualities," the things you value about yourself. Take your time. Think of different people in your life and what qualities they each value about you.

4. List situations that have occurred in your life that seemed to repeat themselves in one way or another. What lesson did you learn from the reoccurrences?

5. Is there an uncomfortable or awkward situation or relationship in your life at the moment? If so, take a deep breath and imagine yourself surrounded by all your power. Imagine facing the situation from this position of indestructible power. What do you see is the action that you need to take? How can you take this action lovingly or with compassion?

6. Think back to situations you may have resolved with anger, unkind words, drama, or force.

Acknowledge that you used the only tools you knew you had at that time. Now that you are realizing your true power, know how differently you will act in the future.

7. Congratulate yourself for your wonderful progress!

"Messages and directives

that focus on separating people

are not coming from a benevolent place."

———◆◆———

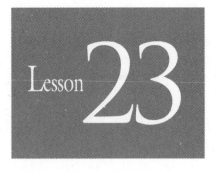

Lesson 23

Share and share alike.

This lesson deals with a subject that has been a cause of confusion for people of many ages, both *through* the ages and for people of different age ranges. I'm talking about the subject of sharing.

Think back to your beginnings. When you were an infant, you were one with all that surrounded you. You were glorious!

Then you were given *things*— a stuffed animal, a toy, an item of clothing — and told they were *yours*. Although you may not be able to recall this period in your life, this made no sense, but you were learning "the rules of the game" of this life and you were all "good sports" to play along. But shortly thereafter, you were told that it was wrong for you to become too possessive of your things — that you were to share these things with your friends and playmates. Now you were confused about how the game was to be played, and about who you were.

Understand that an infant arrives with the knowledge of being totally connected to the wisdom of the universe: totally free, totally loving of everyone and everything. This is indeed the truth to which you as adults aspire today: to re-connect with this universal truth.

Then to be taught that you "own" things — that some things are yours and some things are others' — was very confusing. But you all went along with this teaching, as you were here to learn in whatever way things unfolded. *However, as you were being reprimanded for not sharing, you observed a world in which everyone defined themselves based on their possessions.*

Again, you were confused. And all of you wanted to play by the rules, but the rules became increasingly more confusing.

When you entered school, you were told to have "school spirit," which sounded like a unifying act of solidarity. However, when you realized that your school would compete with other schools, this spirit became the very thing that *separated* you from your opponents. Some of you may have even cheered some unpleasant things to encourage your team to victory. I've heard such cries as, "Trample 'em," "Stomp 'em," and even "Kill 'em"!

You've spent your entire lives bouncing back and forth between illusions. You were told to be part of a unity consciousness (a team, a club, a school, a fraternity/sorority, a company, etc.) which, in fact, was exactly the opposite, because this *illusion of unity* separated you from others and was usually infused with ego and false pride. This illusion presented the message that you (your team, your company, your school ...) were better than others.

Look at your political system. Do you not pit candidates against each other, spending a vast amount of time and energy to determine who is the best? And how do you reach your opinion? From truthful information freely given, or in an endless battle of mud-slinging and name-calling? And this is how you choose your leaders? Please!

I know that the confusion some of you feel now about your true identity and purpose can be tied to this issue of sharing. In trying to figure out what was "yours" and what was not, you determined what is "you." From the many conflicting messages of where you were to put your allegiance, finally you tuned out your brain's frantic efforts to find the truth of your identity and loyalty. It was simply too much effort. You needed to survive.

In short, *you have been trained to fall into the group mindset without questioning it*, as it was too confusing to find the truth. Your brain was exhausted from this subject years ago. So you do not put up a fight. You have been well trained to be the "good soldier."

Being the good soldier, you perform as expected without thinking about the larger picture. However, many of you *have* thought about the larger picture for some time, but be aware that elements of this "good soldier" conditioning have left a great degree of residue. As we have discussed before, messages and directives that focus on separating people are not coming from a benevolent place. And likewise, the same is true of messages aimed at keeping you from embracing your true power.

The more you begin to see and feel how interconnected you all are, the more the confusion will dissipate, the more you will understand and feel TRUE unity consciousness, and the more you will return to the depth of knowledge you had from day one.

So, by sharing and seeing how you are truly all one, you will indeed learn all of the individual facets that compose your unique, wise essence!

Homework:

Write about how you may have been confused about issues that demanded your allegiance to a "group mindset."

When confronted with a situation that separates you from others, how does it make you feel? How do you feel in your body, in your feeling center (in your gut)?

"Your conditioning is being reinforced with much of the entertainment today."

———⊷◆⊶———

Lesson 24

That's entertainment!

We've talked before about how programmed your programming is — in other words, how manipulative your broadcast programming is.

As you are all reclaiming your power and true identity, I wanted to point out one area to be cautious of, an area where you will be instrumental to others in helping them see the magnitude of this situation.

Look at your media. On television and in the movies, you are constantly bombarded with images of people — and especially women — who give away their power. In short, your conditioning is being reinforced with much of the "entertainment" of today.

Think of how people give their power away to television and film personalities. They admire people who are not real, who are just images or illusions. And what qualities make up these "idols"? Are these truly the enlightened beings who possess great wisdom? Or are they admired for how they appear in a bustier or a bandoleer of bullets?

I know you are already aware of how the masses regard "stars," but I don't think you really see how conditioned this truly is. These stars have been formulated to appear as gods, in a way.

Think of it. These "stars" seem to have super-human qualities, in appearance or in strength (though much may be accomplished through the magic of make-up and special effects!). They are omnipresent: you see their images everywhere, from the newspapers to magazines to supermarket tabloids to television, etc.

Some of your serial TV and film characters become "real" in the minds of children or of fans addicted to the shows or films. This, in essence, is creating a virtual reality scenario, as the viewer has taken the storyline as real, perhaps a life he/she would prefer to have over his/her own. So *people aspire to be like them.*

But, most importantly, the most conditioned quality of star-worshipping is that of "imprinting."

When you were an infant, you gazed into your mother's face. That face represented security, love, acceptance, and a total connection. In a way, you saw yourself in your mother's face. *You aspired to be like her.* Her face made a lasting imprint on your identity. You knew then, in some way, that you would grow up to be like her in some respects.

Now, consider when you sit in a darkened movie theater and gaze into a face enlarged on a movie screen. You regress into the acceptance mode of the infant that you were. When a face is in front of you for a period of time, when you are in a mode of just watching and not conversing, you will *worship* that face. It may be an entertainer, a seminar leader, a teacher.

Oftentimes, when people encounter a "star" in person, they instantly feel inferior. They do not feel that they are "on the same level" as the star. This actually has less to do with self-esteem and more to do with imprinting.

So just be aware that anytime that you find yourself admiring others in the public eye, stop for a moment, and consider the wonderful, powerful force that is *you.* And the more you connect with your true essence, the more you let your inner light shine, the more you will feel throughout every cell of your body that YOU are the TRUE STAR!

Homework:

1. Consider the "characters" (either from films or TV) who had an influence on your growth from the time you were a small child. Who did you want to be like? Who did you NOT want to be like and why? Who did you want to look like? How did you want to live? Write down your answer to these questions.

2. Drawing upon your work in earlier lessons, where you identified your strengths and the things that give you joy, what changes in your present life can you make to support and celebrate your "true self" as the "star" in your own "movie"?

"The more you live in line with your true self,

the more you will manifest your dreams."

———⋄◆⋄———

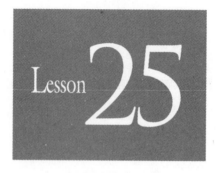

Lesson 25

Manifest destiny.

My dear students,

It seems as though our lessons are coming to an end, at least for now. I am pleased by how you are incorporating all your learning into your daily life. You have grown in ways of which you are not as yet aware. You will continue to do so.

Understand that as you live more and more in line with your true self — your powerful, joyful, creative, unlimited self — you will manifest your dreams. I know that, living in a culture where you were taught to have your dreams as a child and yet to abandon them as a "responsible adult" in favor of making a living in the world, my telling you that you will manifest your dreams may seem a bit hokey. But this is true. And you have already experienced this.

The more you are in line with your innate wisdom and wonderful essence, the more you will feel as though you are "in the flow" of things, or, more appropriately, life. You are in a wonderful connection with the spirit that connects all things in the universe.

When you are in this "flow," you are truly powerful. Then, the gap between thought and action (or "dreaming" and "reality") closes. Things you wish for will suddenly appear in your life. And it will not be a coincidence. Know that you have the power to create your life, your reality, and your dreams. KNOW THIS!

All these lessons to date have been designed to remove energy blocks from your mind and body, to remove these programmed blocks from your awareness so that your energy can truly dance itself alive.

You will feel freer and happier at times than ever before. And what you focus on will carry this new, energized intent. This is how manifesting works.

Be clear in your intent of what you want. Know that you deserve it. Imagine having it and the feeling of having it. The more you can feel this, the more quickly you will be able to manifest your desires.

Treat this process with respect, and it will return the favor. This knowledge carries with it a great responsibility.

So know that it is your destiny to have all that you desire, to be joyful and abundant. This is the truth.

So enjoy this new phase in your life and create wonderful things. All of you are truly manifesting wonderful destinies on the planet now and will do so even more in the future.

I offer my thanks and delight to be a part of this process.

—Jason

ABOUT THE AUTHOR

DEBORAH SOUCEK

Deborah Soucek (so check) has been involved in various aspects of communications for over 20 years. She has worked in advertising and marketing since 1975. Her key interest focuses on the psychological and cultural influences of advertising in our society. In addition, she is the founder of the non-profit organization "Welcome Neighbor!" which offers cross-cultural training and communications to various communities in Southern California. Debbie offers "Navigating" seminars and workshops to both individuals and organizations.

Debbie welcomes your comments and inquiries. Please send your correspondence to her c/o Oughten House at the address shown on page 175 or by direct fax at (805) 297-6022.

About the Publisher and Logo

The name "Oughten" was revealed to the publisher fifteen years ago, after three weeks of meditation and contemplation. The combined effect of the letters carries a vibratory signature, signifying humanity's ascension on a planetary level.

The logo represents a new world rising from its former condition. The planet ascends from the darker to the lighter. Our experience of a dark and mysterious universe becomes transmuted by our planet's rising consciousness — glorious and spiritual. The grace of God transmutes the dross of the past into gold, as we leave all behind and ascend into the millennium.

Publisher's Comment

Our mission and purpose is to publish ascension books and self-empowerment tools for all peoples and all children worldwide.

We currently serve over fifty authors, musicians, and artists. Many of our authors channel such energies as Sananda, Ashtar, Archangel Michael, St. Germain, Archangel Ariel, Serapis, Mother Mary, and Kwan Yin. Some work closely with the Elohim and the angelic realms.They need your support to get their channeled messages to all nations. Oughten House Publications welcomes your interest and petitions your overall support and association in this important endeavor.

We urge you to share the information with your friends, and to join our network of spiritually-oriented people. Our financial proceeds are recycled into producing new ascension books and expanding our distribution worldwide. If you have the means to contribute or invest in this process, then please contact us.

OUGHTEN HOUSE PUBLICATIONS

Our imprint includes books in a variety of fields and disciplines which emphasize our relationship to the rising planetary consciousness. We are also developing a line of beautifully illustrated children's books, which deal with all aspects of spirituality. The list that follows is only a sample of our current offerings. To obtain a complete catalog, contact us at the address shown on page 175.

Ascension Books & Books for the Rising Planetary Consciousness

The Crystal Stair: A Guide to the Ascension, by Eric Klein. A collection of channeled teachings received from Lord Sananda (Jesus) and other Masters, describing the personal and planetary ascension process now actively occurring on our planet. — ISBN 1-880666-06-5, $12.95

The Inner Door: Channeled Discourses from the Ascended Masters on Self-Mastery and Ascension, by Eric Klein. In these two volumes, intended as a sequel to *The Crystal Stair*, the Masters address the challenges of the journey to ascension.

Volume One: ISBN 1-880666-03-0, $14.50

Volume Two: ISBN 1-880666-16-2, $14.50

Jewels on the Path: Transformational Teachings of the Ascended Masters, by Eric Klein. In this book, the ideas and themes introduced in Klein's earlier books are clarified and refined. The reader is brought up to date on what exactly the ascension process consists of and how to be a more active participant in it. Current topics are also discussed. This is the best one yet! — ISBN 1-880666-48-0, $13.50

An Ascension Handbook, by Tony Stubbs. A practical presentation which describes the ascension process in detail and includes several exercises to help you integrate it into your

daily life. Topics include energy and matter; divine expression; love, power, and truth; breaking old patterns; aligning with Spirit; and life after ascension. A best-seller!
— ISBN 1-880666-08-1, $12.95

What Is Lightbody? Archangel Ariel, channeled by Tashira Tachiren. Offers a twelve-level model for the ascension process, leading to the attainment of our Light Body. Recommended in *An Ascension Handbook*, this book gives many invocations, procedures, and potions to assist us on our journey home. Related tapes available. — ISBN 1-880666-25-1, $12.95

The Extraterrestrial Vision: Channeled Teachings from Theodore, channeled by Gina Lake. The mid-causal group entity, Theodore, tells us what we need to know about our extraterrestrial heritage and how to prepare for direct contact with those civilizations which will soon be appearing in our midst. — ISBN 1-880666-19-7, $13.50

Lady From Atlantis, by Robert V. Gerard. Shar Dae, the future empress of Atlantis, is suddenly transported onto a rain-soaked beach in modern-day America. There she meets her twin flame and discovers her mission: to warn the people of planet Earth to mend their ways before Mother Earth takes matters in her own hands! — ISBN 1-880666-21-9, $12.95

Intuition by Design, by Victor R. Beasley, Ph.D. A boxed set of 36 IQ (Intution Quotient) Cards contain consciousness-changing geometrics on one side and a transfomative verse on the other. The companion book tells you the many ways to use the cards in all aspects of your life. An incredible gift to yourself or someone you love. — ISBN 1-880666-22-7, $21.95

Navigating the '90s, by Deborah Soucek. Down-to-earth, practical ways to help yourself make the personal shifts in awareness and behavior required by these accelerated times. Loving and succinct observations and exercises through which we can reclaim our true selves and shed the "programming" of our past. ISBN 1-880666-47-2, $13.95

Angels of the Rays, by Mary Johanna. This book contains portraits of, information about, and messages from twelve different angels who are here to help us in our ascension process. Includes twelve removable full-color Angel Cards and directions for their use. — ISBN 1-880666-34-0, $18.95

My Ascension Journal, by Nicole Christine. Transform yourself and your life by using the journaling methods given in this book. Includes several real-life examples from the author's own journals, plus many blank pages on which to write your own ascension story. This quality-bound edition will become a treasured keepsake to be re-read over and over again. — ISBN 1-880666-18-9, $24.95

Bridge Into Light: Your Connection to Spiritual Guidance, by Pam and Fred Cameron. Lovingly offers many step-by-step exercises on how to meditate and how to channel, and gives ways to invoke the protection and assistance of the Masters. Companion tape available. — ISBN 1-880666-07-3, $11.95

Transformational Tools

We offer an ever-expanding selection of transformational tools to assist you in your journey back to mastery. These include books and tapes, with such titles as *Intuition by Design*, *Heart Initiation*, *Ascending From the Center*, *Ascension: Beginner's Manual*, *The Thymus Chakra Handbook*, *Parallel Realities*, *The Feminine Aspect of God*, *Ascension Merkabah*, *Soul Alignment*, Joshua Stone's books on ascension, and several series of tapes by authors such as Tashira Tachi-ren, Solara, August Stahr, and Crea. Hear the voices and experience the energies of our authors, on companion tapes to *Bridge Into Light* and *The Extraterrestrial Vision*.We also have products such as Ascension Cards to help you focus on your ascension process as it unfolds in your life. For more information on these and other titles in this category, please call or write for our free catalog.

Music Tapes

We carry many titles of spiritually-based music, including both vocal and instrumental types, by artists such as Richard Shulman, Omashar, Stefan Jedland, and Michael Hammer. Create your own "ascension chamber" whenever you play them — at home or wherever your journey takes you. For a listing of available titles, call or write for our free catalog. A reply card is bound into this book for your convenience, or you may reach us at the location listed at the back of this book.

Children's Books and Tapes

Books and tapes in this category include titles such as *Nature Walk, Mary's Lullaby, Song of Gothar, Bear Essentials of Love,* and the "Little Angel" book series. Although primarily intended for children and adults who interact with children, they speak to the "child" within us all.

ATTENTION: BUSINESSES AND SCHOOLS!

OUGHTEN HOUSE books are available at quantity discounts with bulk purchases for educational, business, or sales promotional use. For details, please contact the publisher at the address shown on page 175.

Reader Networking and
Mailing List

The ascension process presents itself as a new reality for many of us on planet Earth. Many seek to know more. Thousands of people worldwide are reaching out to find others of like mind and to network with them. The newly formed Oughten House Foundation stands ready to serve you all.

You have the opportunity to become a member, stay informed, and be on our networking mailing list. Send us the enclosed Information Reply Card or a letter. We will do our best to keep you and your network of friends up to date with ascension-related literature, materials, author tours, workshops, and channelings.

NOTE: If you have a network database or small mailing list you would like to share, please send it along!

Catalog Requests & Book Orders

Catalogs will gladly be sent upon request. For catalogs to be sent outside of the USA, please send $3.00 for postage and handling. Book orders must be prepaid: check, money order, international coupon, VISA, MasterCard, Discover Card, and American Express accepted. Include UPS shipping and handling as follows (no P.O. boxes for UPS):

UPS Domestic Shipping and Handling:

ORDER TOTAL	GROUND	3-DAY	2-DAY	NEXT DAY
$00.01 to $10.00	$ 4.50	$ 6.00	$ 8.25	$16.00
$10.01 to $30.00	$ 5.75	$ 7.25	$10.00	$19.50
$30.01 to $50.00	$ 7.00	$ 8.25	$11.25	$21.00
$50.01 to $70.00	$ 8.50	$10.25	$12.50	$25.00
$70.01 to $100.00	$10.50	$12.50	$14.50	$27.50
$100.01 to $150.00*	$12.50	$15.75	$17.50	$35.00

*All orders over $150.00 need to call for a shipping estimate
*HI, AK, PR orders are shipped Priority Mail or Book Rate
*All continental US orders shipped UPS unless requested otherwise
*Allow 48 hours to process all regular orders

INTERNATIONAL ORDERS:

Charges include actual shipping costs for international Air or Surface Printed Matter, plus an additional $4.00 handling fee.

If paying by check or money order, please use US funds, through a US bank or an International Money Order, payable to Oughten House Publications. Allow approximately 6 weeks for international delivery and 10 working days for US delivery. (Note: Book prices, shipping, and handling charges are subject to change.)

To place your order, call, fax, or mail to:

OUGHTEN HOUSE PUBLICATIONS
P.O. Box 2008
Livermore • California • 94551-2008 • USA
Phone (510) 447-2332
Fax (510) 447-2376

What people are saying about *Navigating the '90s:*

"It so neatly, clearly articulates all life lessons."
— R. Parker
Screenwriter and Producer

"Buckle your seat belt! The changes start so fast. For the first time, I feel I am in the driver's seat of my own life."
— A. Klein
Media Sales Executive

"I've changed from feeling busy, stressed, and incomplete to being right on schedule. I am now an active partici-pant in my life!"
— S. Enay
International Securities Trading Assistant

"Do it in a group! The lessons seem obvious, but to really *live* them will change your life!"
— C. Billups
Facilities Manager